EMOTION AND DEVOTION

The Natalie Zemon Davis Annual Lecture Series
at Central European University, Budapest

EMOTION AND DEVOTION

The Meaning of Mary in Medieval Religious Cultures

Miri Rubin

CEU PRESS

Central European University Press

Budapest – New York

© 2009 by Miri Rubin

Published in 2009 by

Central European University Press
An imprint of the
Central European University Share Company
Nádor utca 11, H-1051 Budapest, Hungary
Tel: +36-1-327-3138 or 327-3000
Fax: +36-1-327-3183
E-mail: ceupress@ceu.hu
Website: www.ceupress.com

400 West 59th Street, New York NY 10019, USA
Tel: +1-212-547-6932
Fax: +1-646-557-2416
E-mail: mgreenwald@sorosny.org

All rights reserved. No part of this publication may be reproduced,
stored in a retrieval system, or transmitted,
in any form or by any means, without the permission
of the Publisher.

Cover design and layout by Péter Tóth
On the cover: Madonna del latte by Paolo di Giovanni Fei, Foto Lensini, Siena.

ISBN 978-968-9776-36-4
ISSN 1996-1197

Library of Congress Cataloging-in-Publication Data
Rubin, Miri, 1956-
Emotion and devotion: the meaning of Mary in medieval religious cultures /
Miri Rubin. p. cm. -- (The Natalie Zemon Davis annual lecture series at Central
European University, Budapest)
Includes bibliographical references and index.
ISBN 978-9639776364 (pbk.: alk. paper)
1. Mary, Blessed Virgin, Saint--Devotion to--Europe--History--To 1500. 2.
Europe--Religious life and customs. I. Title. II. Series.

BT652.E85R83 2009   232.91094'0902--dc22   2008053271

Contents

Preface | 1

Chapter 1. The Global "Middle Ages" | 5

Chapter 2. Mary, and Others | 45

Chapter 3. Emotions and Selves | 79

Index | 111

Preface

I remember very clearly the day on which I was introduced to Natalie Davis's work. It was 1977 and I was an MA student at the Hebrew University of Jerusalem. *Society and Culture in Early Modern France* was only a few months old. So great was the desire of teachers and students to read it, that the imported volume was guarded in a locked room behind the History librarian's chair, a cubicle ominously known as the cage—*hakluv*. Everything about the essays in that volume fulfilled the promise of an article she had written a few years earlier, "Some Tasks and Themes in the Study of Popular Religion."[1] The concepts and historical questions which Natalie Davis set out so eloquently in 1974—gender, popular politics, rituals of violence—still form a challenging framework for research on the religious cultures of Europe. The article's title has helped me to frame this series of lectures which forms part of the celebration in history of a most beloved and revered historian here at Central European University. In that spirit, and based on my work towards a cultural history of the figure of the Virgin Mary, I offer this book which contains somewhat revised versions of the three Natalie Zemon Davis Lectures of 2007. The first chapter—*The Global "Middle Ages"*—considers the historiographical frame for the study of religious cultures and suggests ways in which we may make our practice more global. The second chapter—*Mary, and Others*—examines the polemical situations around Mary, and the location of Muslims and Jews within them. The third, and last, chapter—*Emotions and Selves*—will track the sentimental education experienced by Europeans through devotional encounters with the figure of the Virgin Mary in word, image and sound.

This book has been inspired by the example of another historian, Gábor Klaniczay, whose leadership has helped shape the vision of history practised at the Central European University. With deep erudition and fertile imagination he has explored unknown terrains of European religious experience. He has imbued medieval studies with the passions that animate his life as a foremost public intellectual. These lectures owe a great deal to him, as they do to the generous collegiality of István Perczel, István Rév, Marianne Sághy and to illuminating conversations with György Geréby and to other colleagues too. I am also grateful to Dr. Camilla Russell and Ms. Kati Ihnat for commenting on this work. Linda Kunos of CEU Press has been most helpful and efficient in bringing these lectures to press.

Notes
[1] "Some Tasks and Themes in the Study of Popular Religion," in *The Pursuit of Holiness in Late Medieval and Renaissance Religion*, ed. Charles Trinkaus and Heiko A. Oberman, Leiden, 1974, pp. 307–36.

Chapter 1

The Global "Middle Ages"

I continue to follow the autobiographical strand with which I began. Coming to the world of historical research in the mid-1980s was tantamount to an exhilarating immersion in a gushing fountainhead. So much was fresh and new, and there was more to come. Gender was becoming established as a necessary tool of knowledge and historical understanding; groups traditionally neglected or indeed condescended to by historians—women, peasants, children, artisans, Jews, gypsies, lower clergy—had found their champions too. The tedious claim by some that these groups could not be studied simply because they had left no sources was being countered by the ingenious strategies of determined historians who possessed well-tuned archival antennae: and so, new types of sources were being identified, for the study of lives, feelings, experiences, resistances. Historians almost always encounter these lives through sources produced by bureaucracies and administrations, be they royal, seigneurial or ecclesiastical. There is a truly sensuous delight in eking out of the most unpromising source the stuff of human drama: as Natalie Davis herself has done when working with petitions for pardon to the French king, and another great historian, the late R. W. Scribner, in appreciating cheap and seemingly crude propaganda woodcuts of the early Reformation. Much of this historical enterprise was animated by the desire to give respect, by recovering voices, cherishing experiences, and recounting the suffering.

This capacious history of men and women, high and low, their lives and hopes and fears is here to stay: the materials have been identified and the emergent histories are so subtle and compelling that they are all but becoming the mainstream. The spheres of historical interest are now more integrated than ever before. Where in the past one had to choose whether to look high or low, to choose which domain to inhabit, we now investigate the terrain of encounters, the circumstances of the interaction itself, the shared space: worker and master, owner and slave, husband and wife and children, mystic and confessor, missionary and indigenous people, neighborhoods in their diversity, regions comprising towns and villages. These interactions involve state officials and local communities, law and neighborhood; they can be banal or traumatic. I suggest that the terrain of encounter, with its ingredients of conflict, coercion and difference encompasses the frontier of exacting historical work: criminal and judge, the townsperson and the beggar on the street, the vendor and the purchaser, parent and child. This is a terrain which Natalie Davis has probed and conceptualized, not least in her current project on braided lives.[2]

All these remarkable achievements resulted from a combination in historians of ethical commitment and the imaginative deployment of traditional skills: archival, linguistic, and quantitative. They resulted from the willingness of historians—even before they were labeled *cultural* historians—to open their minds to other disciplines, and to the challenges that these posed. Natalie Davis was a pioneer in harnessing anthropology to historical research; ethnography taught the skills of observation of ritual; literary criticism helped make texts speak against their most obvious grains; feminism and gender theory helped situate the disparate cases of men and women within patterns of sexual politics; social theory offered ways of understanding the interaction between disparate agents within communities. Post-colonial theory came later, theorized both in the Anglo-American academic world and by scholars in countries where the post-colonial was the inescapable reality, to make meaning and history of the experience of colonized people all over the globe. This made historians think—including those researching much earlier periods not touched by modern European colonization—about issues of domination and race, subjugation and conquest, in the First World too.

Another terrain of expansion in cultural history gave pre-modern historians less cause for anxiety—and this is the incorporation of images and the visual into historical work—what we might call the 'visual turn,' led by friendly and welcoming art historians such as Michael Baxendall, Hans Belting and Michael Camille. Unlike the unsettling challenges of seemingly unhistorical "theory," images are reassuringly of the historical period under discussion. They were available to the people of the past in homes, parish churches, on street corners, and were made to be used, "read." The venerable and elegant world of art history, through interaction with literary theory and anthropology, generated its own "new art history," which like the "new history" sought to illuminate the life of the many, their attitudes and mentalities. Some art history moved from the "beautiful" to the "ugly," as Joseph Koerner and Jeffrey Hamburger have starkly named it;[3] from "high quality" to the "low," from the costly to the cheap. The religious art of parishes, hitherto practically untouched by most historians—and long the domain of antiquarians and local historians—came to be studied through its images for common religious instruction and admonition: the Crucifix, the Virgin Mary and Child Christ, the Mouth of Hell. New images were discovered, too, sometimes in unlikely places, "ugly" images, which made women weep in their devotions, or woodcuts, cheap and cheerful.[4] Images and texts, sometimes combined in genres like Books of Hours, chap-books and ballad sheets, required studying by liturgical scholars, historians and art historians leading to fruitful sharing of expertise. Few historians now omit the consideration of visual and material culture; images are used not only as illustrations to the books of historians, they are its very subject matter, as in Eamon Duffy's *The Stripping of the Altars*. The move to expand "downwards" further leads to the enrichment of approaches to those images which have been traditionally deemed elevated. A complex cultural history of religion has revised our understanding of the masters themselves: Grünewald and Botticelli, van der Weyden and Dürer.

The task of understanding life in the pre-modern past has thus become complex and variegated; it incorporates quite habitually wide ranges of sources, often used comparatively, and with telling juxtapositions. A strong sense of the diversity of pre-modern cultures has also emerged—in a Europe of regions—then as now. The Europe of regions is not one of regional isolation or misrecognition between parts. Medieval Europeans were travellers; they journeyed to markets, on pilgrimage, as soldiers, as students, forging marriages and alliances, buying and selling, or just getting away from it all. They were restless Europeans. They travelled and they also returned, sharing tales, experience and expertise. Moreover, they were Europeans in a Eurasian sphere and nowhere is this more evident than in Hungary.

Be it of Europe or Eurasia, that past is increasingly seen as an integrated system—economically, dynastically, and administratively. This was not a

Europe at peace, but it was able to feed its tens of millions, to maintain a vast network of exchange, and to offer a modicum of safety to most people, on the road and in public spaces. It was a culture that habitually imagined its own transformation, through fantasies of purity gained at the price of purging the inner dangers: in different places and at different times these were Jews, heretics, lepers, and witches. Europe was also able to mobilize its resources and enthusiasm against external dangers such as the Mongols or the Turks.[5]

Inasmuch as Europe in the Middle Ages is now understood to be diverse and varied, it remains none the less, bounded by the strong sense of its European, continental destiny. It is still treated as closed. Even though medieval Europe sent missionaries and merchants to large parts of the world then known, even as its demography oscillated in response to disease which traveled from afar, even as its foods, medicines and pigments were made available thanks to the longest possible trade routes, pre-modern Europe is still studied as a sole and separate entity, above all its "Middle Ages." In a brilliant article Timothy Reuter challenged this approach and offered a clear alternative:

> The one substantial alternative on offer—in a number of variant forms—in effect does away with stages of development altogether, and by implication perhaps also with synchronic and diachronic comparison: instead, it attempts to see all human history as a linked whole, with shifting core and hegemonic regions which influenced peripheries not just in the era of increasingly European domination after AD 1500 but long before that.[6]

In her practice, so evident in her books *Women on the Edge* and in her recent *Trickster's Travels*, Natalie Davis, more than any other historian, has attempted to see Europe in just that way.

* * *

How might we experience this reach beyond Europe, this linkedness? In this chapter I shall discuss the possibilities as these became more apparent to me over my years of research and study of the figure of the Virgin Mary.[7] Here I also offer some suggestions of ways in which historians of medieval Europe may develop a practice that is global.

All historians of European religious cultures know a great deal about Mary, but I began to study her more closely when working on Jewish-Christian relations: Marian miracles often had Jewish protagonists; Jews were accused of blasphemy and enmity towards the Virgin Mary; Jews were seen as agents of the Crucifixion, an event which was increasingly seen in later medieval centuries as a drama about Mary; in the wake of late medieval expulsions synagogues were often turned into Marian shrines. The figure of Mary accompanied initiatives of reform and renewal, such as those of Gerson and Savonarola, of Bernardino da Siena and Vincent Ferrer. I became interested in the potent dichotomy between this figure of utmost purity and nurture, and the construction of utmost perversity and pollution in the late medieval Jew, the Jew of conspiracy and desecration, the Jew of treason and blasphemy.

It would have been the easiest thing to write a book on Mary in the Middle Ages, or Mary in the Renaissance; there is so much to be learned and said about both subjects. But I found myself intellectually drawn in other, and new, directions, new to me both in time and in space. One led me backwards, to Mary's life narratives, traditions that emerged in the early Christian centuries. They never gained canonical status as scripture, but circulated widely and persistently as *apocrypha*. These narratives are only slightly younger than the gospels, and they provided an utterly necessary set of answers to questions about the circumstances of Christ's birth and background, through the life of his mother. This story of Mary's emergence in the Near East at the dawn of Christianity is an interesting and instructive part of the history that saw Mary reach in European cultures the heights of ubiquitous and much-cherished devotion.

And so from medieval Europe—my starting point—I was led to study the creation, translation and dissemination of stories about the Jewish maiden who bore God. Besides the accounts of the Gospels—above all Matthew and Luke with their narratives of Annunciation and Nativity—there was the text of the mid-second century, *The Protogospel of James,* which filled in the gaps in the Gospel stories, working out "their logical implications."[8] This spurred me to engage with the earliest poetry on Mary, Syriac poetry, and with the making of the story of Mary's end, the Dormition, followed by her Assumption; it led me to consider the powerful political and cultural milieu of emergent imperial Christianity, which produced a majestic and hieratic, frontal and penetrating image of Mary. Here was a blend of feminine imperial iconography with the power of Mary as Bearer of God, as she came to be officially known from the time of the Council of Ephesus (431), though this elevation of Mary was not to the liking of many Christians, like those in the eastern, Syriac regions.[9] Additionally, there was an Egyptian influence in the making of Mary, one that emphasized Mary's maternity, her nurturing breast. Images of Mary drew upon the tradition of Isis, especially in Egypt. When Christianity came to dominate in Upper Egypt some Isis temples were turned into churches dedicated to the Mother of God. Isis was perceived as fecund, curing and protective; Mary was the woman who bore a God and brought salvation into the world.

So a medievalist became immersed in the materials and concerns of peoples in the centuries of intricate interaction between Judaism, Christianity and Pagan religions. These concerns were well beyond the familiar terrain of an historian of the Middle Ages, and yet they were so vital to the questions raised by involvement with medieval religious cultures. The interest in the making of Mary thus provided a prompt that we may call "global," inasmuch as it goes beyond the period and place of the imagined medieval. Global is an orientation in space that draws in other parts of the world, beyond that which is most immediately suggested. Global may also mean that glances at the European continent are challenged, so as to include, or indeed reorient study towards regions otherwise treated as marginal and peripheral.

Let us think of a few examples. The study of the cult of the Virgin Mary is most usually associated by medieval historians with the regions of Western Europe, with centers such as Rocamadour, Chartres and Loreto, with Romanesque facades, Gothic statues and Early Renaissance icons; with the poetry of Gautier de Coinci and Dante. When we find examples of the cult in areas outside the center, these are usually treated as examples of "influence," and this implies subordination, or marginality. Yet the move inspired by Robert Bartlett in his *The Making of Europe,* suggests ways in which the very zone on which influence is brought to bear—through conquest, missions or trade—becomes the sphere of creativity and definition.[10] Periphery becomes center, provincial avant-garde.

This vision may be developed as a "global" insight whereby we identify particular creativity in the process of encounter implied in, say, the adoption of the cult of Mary in millennium Hungary, or the use of the Gothic in Prague, or the making of Icelandic versions of Marian miracle tales. Gábor Klaniczay has demonstrated compellingly how around the end of the first millennium the Hungarian Christian dynasty adopted and adapted the cult of Mary into the political culture of their nascent sacred kingdom.[11] This was part of a move towards political autonomy and hegemony, one that situated the kingdom in a newly defined position between the Byzantine imperial and Holy Roman imperial spheres. The Virgin was chosen as the kingdom's patron and protector; liturgy and ceremony centered on her and soon artifacts and spaces were made, inspired by her shape and qualities. Where did the political theology of Mary come from? King Stephen of Hungary—St Stephen—was as much aware of Byzantine courtly traditions as he was of the Marian devotion of Adalbert, the missionary who had made Hungary Christian.

A globalizing sensibility would encourage us to see the world from Stephen's point of view: to appreciate with him and his advisors the potential embedded in the figure of Mary, a figure which transcended political contingency, and was unrivalled by any other saint. Another political-religious entity, the congregations associated with Cluny Abbey, was moving in a similar direction. There, too, a new formation was created, linked to the patronage of a great lord, and to the devotional tastes and lifestyle that suited the social class that produced cohorts of monks. Originally hubs of liturgy and intercession, Cluniac houses developed into centers of political influence throughout western Europe. Here, too, something about the cult of Mary was appreciated, long before Europeans began to transform Mary into the immaculately pure ever-present nurturing mother, the Madonna of every street-corner of later centuries. Her majesty and her purity, her universal status—unlike local saints and cherished martyrs—made her an emblem for the new enterprise that radiated from the mother-house in Burgundy and under the auspices of the papacy in Rome. Taken together, the moves made towards Mary by the King of Hungary and by the leaders of the Cluniac congregation seem more akin than apart, more alike than not. They suggest that events at the "center" and the "periphery" are often best looked at in different combinations, within globalizing frames that suggest comparison where such had never been attempted before.

If we take a "global" approach to the adoption of Mary, we see the qualities of a cult—in this case of the

Virgin Mary—through use and application. Moreover, as we consider Cluny and Hungary both, and their sources of inspiration—in ideas, liturgy and art—we are struck by an intricate affinity: both shared important and defining relations with the imperial court at Aachen, itself a polity closely bound dynastically and culturally to the mother of all imperial Christianity, Byzantium. So we have come full circle, and as a circle is without beginning or end, so must the process we describe be without centers and peripheries. The global turn subverts the hierarchy within Europe and reveals the flows of encounters and influences which are to historians both intriguing and suggestive. As to the interest in Mary, cherished in both places, at opposite ends of Europe, here is a precocious appreciation of the qualities which were to be widely and forcefully valued in the following centuries; the cult of Mary *avant la letter*.

* * *

By engaging with the rich materials of the early centuries I sought to understand how this figure of Mary—quintessentially of the eastern Mediterranean—came to be the ubiquitous spiritual companion of monks, pilgrims and then of parishioners all over Europe.

Some eight years of research have truly tested my training as a medievalist. Medieval historians treasure their ability to engage directly with their sources: to be able to read them from manuscript or authoritative edition, to appreciate genre fully, to have the languages necessary for reading the pertinent secondary literatures. Medieval historians are trained to attain a certain degree of self-sufficiency in skills, more perhaps than historians of other periods. We expect to be able to sustain conversations with medievalists around the world, and with writers of the past in the many languages and styles in which medieval sources were written. We expect to be able to assess a wide range of genres, and to possess interdisciplinary awareness; the Medieval Studies program at the Central European University is a good example of that vision.

Yet the more capacious the theme we address—and the growth of the figure of Mary is a capacious one indeed—the more inadequate our training appears to be. We are forced to rely on the expertise of others; several scholars have turned in the last decade to projects of co-authorship, as one solution to the dilemma. In the course of my research on Mary I have depended on translations from medieval Hungarian, from Armenian, from Ethiopian and Croatian, and more. So the application of a more global methodology results in discomfort within the historian, a rethinking of the relation between historical curiosity and intellectual authority which traditionally draws on a specific set of technical and analytical skills.

The challenge is not only related to linguistic capacities. Studying Mary led me to the world of liturgy, music and song. Mary is song, from the moment of the Visitation, when she (or some would have it Elizabeth) burst into a song of praise—the *Magnificat*. Her praises have been expressed poetically and rhythmically from the hymns of Ephrem the Syrian to the *kontakia* of Romanos and on to the tradition of the *Akathistos*, later to the Latin *Salve Regina* and the chants of confraternities. The hitherto relatively silent Middle Ages, became for me a place of vibrant sound—in liturgy, prayer and communal singing.

Historians have inhabited the silent world of text for too long, but this is changing very fast. With the guidance of historians of music and liturgy—Susan Boynton, Margot Fassler, Anne Walters Robertson, Craig Wright—the history of religious life is becoming engaged with sound as well as imagery.

Architectural spaces offered not only surfaces for decoration—in painting, and carving—but spaces within which sound reverberated according to careful routines. In Christopher Page, historians find a historian of music who is also an accomplished performer; thanks to him we can appreciate the ways in which Hildegard of Bingen (d. 1179) celebrated the Incarnation as a musical happening within Mary's body, in her antiphon *Ave generosa*. In another antiphon, *Splendidissima gemma*, Hildegard explores the power of light:

> Resplendent jewel and unclouded brightness
> of the sunlight streaming through you,
> know that the sun is a fountain leaping
> from the father's heart,
> his all-fashioning word.
> He spoke and the primal matrix
> teemed with things unnumbered—
> but Eve unsettled them all.
>
> To you the father spoke again
> but this time
> the word he uttered was a man
> in your body.
> Matrix of light! through you he breathed forth

all that is good,
as in the primal matrix he formed
all that is life.[12]

This spirited translation provided by Barbara Newman is another example of historical work that is multifaceted and audacious, and which brings light and sound to the Middle Ages. The possibilities inherent in and conveyed by music for the understanding of the religious cultures with Mary at their hearts are a new challenge to us all.

It is customary to think of liturgical music as a quintessential facet of medieval religion and one reduced, if not abolished, in Protestant Christianity. Yet one of the spheres of continuity and indeed dependence on tradition was that of the music associated with the feasts of Mary. Indeed, Luther appreciated the musical Mary lore greatly, above all the *Magnificat*.[13] No one wrote as movingly as Luther about the biblical moments of Mary's life, as in his translation and commentary on the *Magnificat*, 1521:

> Now I do not know in all the Scriptures anything that so well serves such a purpose as this sacred hymn of the most blessed Mother of God,

> which ought indeed to be learned and kept in mind by all who would rule well and be helpful lords. Truly she sings in it most sweetly of the fear of God, what manner of lord He is, and especially what His dealings are with those of high and of low degree. ...It is a fine custom, too, that this canticle is sung in all the churches daily at vespers, and to a particular and appropriate setting that distinguishes it from the other chants.[14]

Indeed, there was real appreciation of song's power to construct and to elevate. To familiar melodies were now attached new words, in an attempt to infuse hymns with the message of scripture and an evangelical vision. Luther envisaged the reformed mass as being full of song, and helped make it so:

> I also wish that we had as many songs as possible in the vernacular which the people could sing during mass... For who doubts that everybody sang these songs originally, which the choir now sings or responds to while the bishop is consecrating?[15]

Luther imagined Protestants participating in music in a familiar vernacular. Such song mirrored the personal responsibility and unmediated access to scripture which were so central to the reformed vision. English Protestant churches also became spaces for the chanting of psalms and congregational hymnody. This too is the historian's terrain.

So the medievalist is drawn to a wide range of sources to be considered historically, looks back in time to origins, and is drawn forward too. Momentous changes in ideas about and representations of Mary took place in the sixteenth century, just across the boundaries observed by most medievalists—the year 1500. For as Europe witnessed the dawn of a new century, religious communities engaged anew with Mary. Mary's place in late medieval religious culture became both varied and ubiquitous, it also became increasingly vexing, tendentious, and disturbing. As Mary soared, so did worries about her proper status within the religious culture. Was religion becoming too "marianised"? Were there too many feasts? Was she immaculately conceived? Was it proper to present her as queen when scripture told of a birth in a manger?

Early in the last century the Dutch scholar Johann Huizinga created a powerful and enduring image of the later Middle Ages as a period marked by the expectation of infantile excitation, instability of spirit, and inherent desire for change for its own sake. None of these stereotypes is made any better by the fact that sometimes a gesture is made towards the Middle Ages, when the term Renaissance is expanded so as colonize the oeuvres of Giotto and Dante and Christine de Pisan, of the Pisani brothers and even Chaucer; similarly when the Reformation is cast so as to include phenomena such as "early Reformation" Wycliffism, Hussitism, or indeed the *Devotio Moderna*. The Middle Ages become shorter, millions of lives and letters are deemed less medieval, but that is only to make the others more intensely "medieval" as a new "ending" is drawn, where? in 1300? in 1250? At the same time many scholars have begun to use years as denominators, 1200–1600, 1400–1600—rather than "medieval" or "late medieval"—to describe their books and courses. It is interesting to experiment with the excision of the term "medieval" in favor of alternative periods of years that make sense for the investigation of a particular problem.

When the medievalist follows through into the sixteenth century, many familiar concerns come into very sharp relief. Europe was about to become a battleground in which images and liturgies were both the subject and the symbolic articulations of aggression. But communities also tolerated and accommodated, and above all re-formulated, like the Lutherans who retained scripture-based feasts, and even some hymns.[16] Images made in the medieval centuries by medieval artists for medieval patrons—individuals, groups or institutions—were being assessed afresh by Protestant eyes: some were destroyed, some were "corrected," others were left for continued use.[17] The very mood of polemic that engaged Europeans—in universities, church councils, as well as in neighborhoods—was bound to keep alive knowledge of the traditions of religious life, even as these were being lampooned and derided. So, for example, the play performed in Evangelical Bern around 1518, aimed at deriding the shrine at Oberbüren, so famed for its powers to revive stillborn babies, described the rituals of pilgrimage in detail even as it mocked the female pilgrims and excoriated their faith.[18] The medieval continued to be performed as polemic, and to adorn, indeed contain, the spaces of worship of Protestant religious life.

Some Protestant female poets turned Mary into a potential sinner, like themselves. Brought down to earth she offered a model to women because like them she had striven to avoid the many sins which loomed and tempted. Reworking the medieval theme of sorrowful and affective concentration on Mary's pain, the English poet Amelia Lanyer (1569-1645) resolved her sorrow into a providential note of joy. In Lanyer's "The Salutation and Sorrow of the Virgine Mary," she reworks the tradition of *mater dolorosa*, one bound so closely to the memory of Jewish guilt:

> When spightfull men with torments did oppresse
> Th'afflicted body of this innocent Dove,
> Poore women seeing how much they did transgresse,
> By teares, by sighes, by cries intreat, nay prove,
> What may be done among the thickest presses,
> They labour till these tyrants hearts to move;
> In pitie and compassion forebeare
> Their whipping, spurning, tearing of his haire.
>
> But all in vaine, thie malice hath no end,
> Their hearts more hard than flint, or marble stone;
> Now to his griefe, his greatnesse they attend,
> When he (God knows) had rather be alone;
> They are his guard, yet seeke all meanes to offend:
> Well may he grieve, well may he sigh and groane,
> Under the burthen of a heavy crosse,
> He faintly goes to make their gaine his losse.

> His woefull Mother wayting on her Sonne,
> All comfortlesse in depth of sorrow drowned;
> Her griefes extreame, although but new begun,
> To see his bleeding body oft shee swooned;
> How could shee choose but thinke her selfe undone,
> He dying, with whose glory shee was crowned?
> None ever lost so great a losse as shee,
> Being Sonne, and Father and Eternitie.[19]

The medieval institutions of council and papacy, of activist bishops and reforming preachers, were all deployed in response to the Protestant challenges. The Council of Trent led the initiatives for Catholic renewal. As Olivier Christin and Philip Soergel have shown, shrines and relics, among them many associated with Mary, were now treated forensically, examined and documented anew. Like their Protestant equivalents, some were retained, and some discarded under the bright light of scrutiny. By the seventeenth century tasks of listing and describing the heritage were imagined, like that of the Jesuit Wilhelm Gumppenberg, who sought to create an atlas of Marian shrines—*atlas marianus*. At the meeting of the Order in 1649 for the election of the Jesuit Master General he distributed 600 copies of an outline—a mission statement *Idea Atlantis Mariani*—and 266 informants sent in returns, with letters and sketches, detailing shrines and images. Gumppenberg sought accurate, almost tangible evidence of the antiquity, shape, and historicity of such shrines, in the face of derision and abuse. This resulted in the *Atlas Marianus sive de imaginibus deiparae per orbem Christianum miraculosis*.[20] Although the cult of Mary was flourishing in the Americas and in parts of Asia, his was a European compilation; Gumppenberg's view was less global than our own interests are now.

* * *

So the cultural history of Mary directed me both backwards and forwards from the terrain of the medieval historian. Yet as the dramas of religious polemic and strife were enacted in large parts of sixteenth-century Europe—and these were struggles over political control of the routes to salvation—Mary reached new domains. While she was tested in Europe—rejected by some, embraced by others—Mary was also becoming a truly global figure, as knowledge of her reached all known continents. Here were whole new vistas and challenges to the figure of Mary and its uses. But is this the terrain of historians trained to understand the medieval centuries? Is this the terrain of the historians of Europe?

Yes. It is, and it must be. The emergent global Mary revealed to me several new potentialities of a medievalist's work, for it was the late-medieval Mary that reached the Canaries, West Africa and Goa in the fifteenth century. Medieval Mary traveled to new places with the extension of Christian religious cultures westwards as part of the enterprises of trade, conquest and mission initiated by European rulers, above all, those of Spain. The late-medieval Mary of shrine and miracle—and in her Iberian form, so pure and sometimes immaculate—was offered to the bruised and shattered survivors of the encounter with Cortes's men, the builders of a New Spain. Franciscan and some Dominican friars were accustomed to teaching Mary to Europeans, to people who were reared on Mary at hearth and home. For centuries they had directed their sermons and the images of their churches to people who had learned about Mary at their mother's knee, from the rhythms of family life and parish religiosity. They knew what to expect—doubt, jokes, sarcasm, incredulity. The new task in worlds new brought them in touch with people without such immersion in a Christian culture from the cradle. Here were new challenges aplenty, and the techniques applied were the tried and tested combination of making familiar and vernacular the narratives of Christianity. These had served friars in Europe; they were to serve them in care of the traumatized New Christians.

And so an avenue for deploying the medievalist's knowledge in a global setting became apparent, and it led me beyond Europe. The realization, so simple yet so rarely acknowledged, that the techniques of missions and conquest, were forged in the "medieval" centuries, was a revelation and a welcome one at that. It meant that medieval historians could contribute to the task of decoding and appreciating the emergent global religious cultures. Like Columbus and Luther, the Franciscans of New Spain are best understood within the traditions of medieval religious cultures and the politics of European courts.

A barrage of conflicting influences assailed the men who were charged with the task of bringing Christianity to the people of Mexico.[21] The dozen Franciscans, who arrived in Vera Cruz in 1524, were an apostolic group geared towards mission.[22] These friars possessed a developed Marian sensibility linked with themes of Passion and compassion, in words and images. Their habits of thought, prayer and contemplation were deeply touched by association with Mary. The music they brought, which served as a tool of mission, was inspired by the polyphony of the Burgundian court, as it had been adapted and developed by the Spanish court.

In New Spain they used some of the skills honed in Old Europe: accommodation to local idioms, provision of useful examples in texts and images, and preaching in the language of the people they sought to convert. The great difference was that in New Spain the friars were very few indeed and the people they aimed to convert were many. They devised a new type of church to accommodate the multitudes coerced and enticed into the new religion. These were open chapels in walled courtyards with a large cross in the middle and a central chapel facing the courtyard. While people assembled in the courtyard they could hear and watch the services conducted in the central chapel. This is where most Mexicans first encountered Mary displayed and celebrated.[23]

The materials which such men offered to the indigenous people, to the new Christians of New Spain, were those most common in European instruction within parishes, at the core of devotional lore. An excellent example is the use of narratives about the Virgin Mary, presented in images and tales above all, just as they were in Europe. Louise Burkhart has studied Codex 7 of the John Carter Brown Library Collection, a book of Marian miracles in Nahuatl. The tales were chosen from the hundreds which were composed and compiled in the Middle Ages—some of which we will examine in Chapter 2—and were translated for the use of recent converts. Originally the work of monks in the twelfth, and of friars from the thirteenth century, Marian tales told of interventions in the daily lives of Europeans. These were consoling, and even more often chastising encounters. Mary showed herself an appreciative recipient of even a single act of good faith in a Christian's lifetime, and a vengeful chastiser of those who wantonly ignored the possibilities of her grace. By the early sixteenth century, works for parish instruction and devotional poetry and tale traveled with the bearers of Christianity to new peoples and places, the genres available in most European vernaculars: English and French, German and Icelandic, Galician and Catalan. In Mexico these were soon remade in the native tongue, Nahuatl. The process of translation is always one of interpretation, and so it was when European tales of a powerful female figure, protective and seemingly all-knowing, were translated and offered in a new language to people who knew female goddesses and powerful matriarchs too.

The contents of the collection are of great interest to medieval scholars, even we who have no knowledge of the language in which it is written. For access to the contents we must rely on Burkhardt's considerable expertise, but once we have gained access to the material through her guidance we discover a very interesting array of highly familiar narratives, which none the less possess emphases and turns of phrase that ring unfamiliar. The collection was based largely on the *Scala Coeli* by the Dominican preacher Johannes Gobi the Younger who was active in the 1330s.[24] They were called *tlamahuizolli*—stories of events that stir wonder and awe—an indigenous genre, which easily absorbed the rich tradition of miraculous tales rendered as didactic *exempla* in medieval Europe.

Here is an opportunity for collaboration and for rediscovery too. For if scholars of medieval religious culture are familiar with the miraculous lore of Mary, they will encounter it afresh, in the versions created by Europeans, scholars working in the lands and languages of their mission. As they translated they also assessed: what belonged quintessentially to the tale, what could be made to fit the Nahua social reality and states of mind, as they understood these to be. Conversely, they were recasting European habits of mind and emphases that had served for centuries. Mary emerges familiar yet new; de-familiarization, as ever, offers insight into that hitherto considered familiar.

Dealing with medieval Marian tales, the product of long centuries of translation and transmission, often from Greek originals, in their post-medieval forms, in languages no medieval historian can understand, is a challenge, but also an opportunity. For medieval scholars have become quite expert at appreciating religious cultures in practice, in the plenitude of their many registers, echoes and possibilities. Indeed, the Nahuatl scholar Daniel Mosquera found reading the work of Aron Gurevich on medieval popular culture to be conceptually helpful.[25] The friars who penned the materials for instruction were few and their task was vast; they confronted a traumatized society and were obliged to learn new languages and come to understand the social mores of an unfamiliar world to which Europeans were both attracted and repelled. Yet their preoccupations with the use of the vernacular in speaking sacred truths, with the use of dramatic devices to attract their audience, with the accommodation of non-Christian traditions into a new local religion—all of these—were dilemmas lived by the priesthood and the friars of Europe too, at all times, and very explicitly in the late medieval centuries.

Mary was remade in the parishes of New Spain into a goddess of fertility and protection. She was much more prominent in expressions of indigenous religious sentiment—when we can consider them from this distance—than was the figure of Christ. Just as in Europe Mary was celebrated not only in universal liturgies, but in myriad local manifestations of her power through images deemed holy.[26] In the diocese of Chiapas there was Our Lady of the Rosary in Copanahuastla, guarded and served by a confraternity since its foundation on the Feast of the Purification 1561. The image was famed for its powers to cure the sick and dying. Like its European counterparts—French, Iberian, Bavarian—this rural cult attracted pilgrims and dispensed solace.[27] Like so many apparitions of Mary in Europe, colonial America produced visionaries who imagined justice and comfort through encounters with Mary.[28]

In these regions of mission and conquest we can also observe the seeds of discipline. Friars worried about the presence of figures of Mary in far-flung parishes served by native Christian priests: these had not been reared at the mother's knee, their minds had not been habituated to Mary of story and miracle by a profusion of images in churches and marketplans. Fears of mis-possession and error were more evident in this world where social life did not provide the local, vernacular, familial context for a Mary of tale and song. But they were not absent from Old Europe where Mary seemed vulnerable and open to abuse in the imagined attitudes of Jews, and later in those of Protestants. Outside the comfort zone of ineluctable absorption in Mary, the clergy developed a more disciplining attitude to her. The encounters raised a mirror in which 1500 years of solace and ineffable possession of and through Mary are reflected sharply.

Historians of Europe have a great deal to learn and also to offer as the traditional borders around historical investigation soften. David Abulafia, a historian of trade in the Mediterranean, now traces his merchants and mariners into the Atlantic, in a book on the earliest encounters in the Canaries, Caribbean and Mexico. Sharon Farmer, a historian of the Parisian poor, is studying the transmission of patterns and know-how from Syria to the silk guilds of that great city. In her recent book Sabina MacCormack combines her understanding of early Christianity with the history of Mexico and Peru in a study of religion, conversion and empires. The literary scholar David Wallace has mapped the literary products of contact with non-Europeans in his elegant *Premodern Places*.[29] The possibilities are many. Medieval people, artifacts and ideas ought not to be bounded by geographic borders, upon which, in any case, we are rarely able to agree. There is a global Middle Ages, and pre-modern historians have a great deal to contribute to the public conversations of our global world.

Notes

[1] Some of these thoughts were developed by me in the Timothy Reuter Lecture 2006.
[2] In Natalie Zemon Davis's forthcoming book.
[3] Jeffrey Hamburger, "To Make Women Weep: Ugly Art as 'Feminine' and the Origins of Modern Aesthetics," *Res* 31 (1997), pp. 9–33; Joseph Koerner is the editor of the issue and contributed an introduction to it.
[4] Ursula Weekes, *Early Engravers and their Public: the Master of the Berlin Passion and Manuscripts from Convents in the Rhine-Maas Region, ca. 1450–1500*, Turnhout, 2004.
[5] Norman Housley, *Religious Warfare in Europe, 1400–1536*, Oxford, 2002, especially chapters 3 and 5.
[6] In Timothy Reuter, *Medieval Polities and Modern Mentalities*, ed. Janet L. Nelson, Cambridge, 2006, pp. 19–37; at p. 36 [first published as *Medieval History Journal* 19(1998), pp. 25–45].
[7] See Miri Rubin, *Mother of God: a History of the Virgin Mary*, London, 2009.
[8] Averil Cameron, *Christianity and the Rhetoric of Empire: the Development of Christian Discourse*, Berkeley (CA), 1991, p. 104.
[9] On these issues see Kate Cooper, "Empress and *Theotokos*: Gender and Patronage in the Christological Controversy," in *The Church and Mary: Papers Read at the 2001 Summer Meeting and the 2002 Winter Meeting of the Ecclesiastical History Society*, ed. R. N. Swanson, Woodbridge, 2004, pp. 39–51.
[10] Robert Bartlett, *The Making of the Middle Ages: Conquest, Colonization and Cultural Change, 950–1350,* London, 1994.
[11] Gábor Klaniczay, *Holy Rulers and Blessed Princesses. Dynastic Cults in Medieval Central Europe,* trans. Éva Pálmai, Cambridge, 2002, pp. 139–42.

12 O splendidissima gemma
et serenum decus solis
qui tibi infusus est,
fons saliens
de corde Patris,
quod est unicum Verbum suum,
per quod creavit
mundi primam materiam,
quam Eva turbavit.

Hoc Verbum effabricavit tibi
Pater hominem,
et ob hoc es tu illa lucida materia
per quam hoc ipsum Verbum exspiravit
omnes virtutes,
ut eduxit in prima materia
omnes creaturas.

Saint Hildegard of Bingen, *Symphonia*, trans. Barbara Newman, Ithaca (NY) and London, no. 10, pp. 114–15.

13 Eyolf Østrem, "Luther, Josquin and *des fincken gesang*," in *The Arts and Cultural Heritage of Martin Luther*, ed. Eyolf Østrem, Jens Fleischer and Nils Holger Petersen, Copenhagen, 2003, pp. 51–79.

14 http://www.godrules.net/library/luther/NEW1luther_c5.htm

15 Martin Luther, *An Order of Mass and Communion*, trans. Paul Zeller Strodach, Philadelphia (PA), 1965, p. 35; on Luther and hymnody see Carl Axel Aurelius, "*Quo verbum dei vel cantu inter populos maneat:* The Hymns of Martin Luther," in *The Arts and Cultural Heritage of Martin Luther*, ed. Eyolf Østrem,

Jens Fleischer and Nils Holger Petersen, Copenhagen, 2003, pp. 19–34.

[16] Beth Kreitzer, *Reforming Mary: Changing Images of the Virgin Mary in Lutheran Sermons of the Sixteenth Century*, Oxford, 2004.

[17] Joseph Leo Koerner, *The Reformation of the Image*, London, 2004; and on Mary, Bridget Heal, *The Cult of Mary in Reformation Germany*, Cambridge, 2007.

[18] Glenn Ehrstine, "Motherhood and Protestant Polemics: Stillbirth in Hans von Rüte's *Abgötterei* (1531)," in *Maternal Measures: Figuring Caregiving in the Early Modern Period*, ed. Naomi J. Miller and Naomi Yavneh, Aldershot, 2000, pp. 121–34.

[19] The "Salutations" form part of Lanyer's 1611 volume *Salve Deus Rex Iudaeorum*; see Isabella Whitney, Mary Sidney and Aemilia Lanyer, *Renaissance Women Poets*, ed. Danielle Clarke, London, 2000, pp. 205–74; at p. 257, lines 993–1016.

[20] 2 vols., Ingolstadt, 1657. I learned a great deal from attending Professor Christin's seminar session at the Institute of Historical Research.

[21] For a subtle analysis of these, as a process of "occidentalization" see Serge Gruzinski, "Occidentalisation," in *La pensée métisse*, Paris, 1999, pp. 87–104.

[22] See image of the arrival of the Franciscans in the Description of Tlaxcala *c.* 1583–5, Serge Gruzinski, *Painting the Conquest: the Mexican Indians and the European Imagination*, trans. Deke Dusinberre, Paris, 1992, p. 44, figure 28.

[23] John Leddy Phelan, *The Millennial Kingdom of the Franciscans in the New World*, second edn., Berkeley (CA), 1970, p. 50.

[24] Louise M. Burkhart, "'Here is another marvel': Marian miracle narratives in a Nahuatl manuscript," in *Spiritual Encoun-*

ters: Interactions between Christianity and Native Religions in Colonial America, ed. Nicholas Griffiths and Fernando Cervantes, Birmingham, 1999, pp. 91–115; on the genre see pp. 95–9; for the Latin original see Jean Gobi, *Scala Coeli*, Marie-Anne Polo de Beaulieu, Paris, 1991.

[25] Daniel Mosquera, "Nahutal Catechistic Drama: New Translations, Old Preoccupations," in *Nahuatl Theater I: Death and Life in Colonial Nahua Mexico,* ed. Barry D. Sell and Louise M. Burkhart, Norman (OK), 2004, pp. 55–84; esp. pp. 56–7.

[26] For images and local cults see Jane Garnett and Gervase Rosser, "The Virgin Mary and the People of Liguria: Image and Cult," *Studies in Church History* 39(2004), pp. 280–97.

[27] Amos Megged, *Exporting the Catholic Reformation: Local Religion and Early-Colonial Mexico,* Leiden, 1996, p. 135.

[28] Nora E. Jaffary, *False Mystics: Deviant Orthodoxy in Colonial Mexico,* Lincoln (NE), 2004; William A. Christian Jr., *Apparitions in Late Medieval and Renaissance Spain,* Princeton (NJ), 1989.

[29] David Abulafia, *The Discovery of Mankind: Atlantic Encounters in the Age of Columbus,* London and New Haven (CN), 2008; Sabine MacCormack, *On the Wings of Time: Rome, the Incas, Spain, and Peru,* Princeton (NJ), 2007; David Wallace, *Premodern Places: Calais to Surinam, Chaucer to Aphra Behn,* Oxford, 2004.

Chapter 2

Mary, and Others

In her article "The rites of violence" Natalie Davis taught many important lessons.[1] One of the most influential was the link she demonstrated and explored between violence and the making of identity. In the course of violent encounters between Catholics and Protestants in sixteenth-century France people acted as bearers and protectors of religious symbols. They were actors in street dramas, and they expressed their identities through the enactment of violence that was patterned and encoded, as rituals are. Inasmuch as people imagined themselves not only as adherents, but as champions and defenders of a pattern of life which included relations with the sacred, they also possessed a sense of the very practice or person which seemed to mock or threaten them. Scholarship on the Middle Ages has been much energized by this insight, combined with the anthropological approach that has taught us to analyze the deep structures and patterns, indeed, the ritual aspect of violence in thoughts and deeds. Identity was expressed and reinforced—and could also be called into question—in the course of participation in violent action.

Identity is a subject with which all historians must grapple.[2] Practitioners of women's history and the history of gender have made formative contributions to thinking historically about identity, as have post-colonial theorists, and literary scholars, often informed by psychoanalysis. All these approaches share the sense of identity as being not a "natural" attribute determined by biology or even by an overriding social condition, such as class or gender. Most historians would agree that identity is the product of nurture and experience, and that it displays some of the learned traits of local cultures. Yet historians and scholars of literature are also aware of the unexpected and the creative elements which identities can display. Moreover, identity can change over a lifetime, and is marked by the accumulation of affinities. It is never static.

Mary was central to the identification and lives of medieval people in many different ways. There was the monk whose life of liturgical action and inner struggle found solace and inspiration in the Virgin Mary. There were nuns whose devotions were particularly attached to Mary as Christ's bride, and as Virgin, and other nuns who favored the fantasy of motherhood through immersion in Mary's own. There were dynasts who saw in Mary exalted royalty, and the promise of dynastic fecundity and health; and there was neighborhood Mary, at street-corners and in parish churches. This loving mother reminded people of the code of Christian life to which they must adhere and in which they so often failed. So much of the Christian story was told through the life of Mary that she became the quintessential symbol of Christian life: this meant that her enemies were those of every Christian.

Thinking about Mary and identity suggests to me at least three modes by which the making of identity operates. We may describe these as agonistic, specular, and related to trauma.
- The *agonistic* involves the emergence of identity through struggle, antagonism with a clearly identified and constructed persona.
- The *specular* involves a relationship of mirroring, sometimes inversion, and is characterized

by the use of binary language, often in a polemical situation.
- *Trauma* and separation characterize identity prompted by return to a single event, place or person, associated with loss, pain or separation. The incursion into a life of a charismatic influence also renders the world different forever.

If identity is something that shifts and changes, which displays itself differently in changing environments, then some mental images may help us to imagine that diversity: clusters and layers.

* * *

Having considered the shapes of identity let us move on to ways in which historians have attempted to explain the emergence of collective orientations in medieval Europe, something akin to identity. The year 1000 has often been used as a watershed; in the eleventh and twelfth centuries economic and political trends favored the formation of a more integrated Europe, and within that world more attention was paid to the formulation of the habits, rituals and symbols of a European *societas christiana.* This also meant that categories such as "Jew," "heretic," and "beguine" were each now explored not as natural categories, but as discursive creations, the product of reflections and actions that are full of purpose and intent. Most famously, in his *Formation of a Persecuting Society*, R. I. Moore associated the construction of the category of "heresy," within a legal framework that identified, persecuted and punished heretics, with the efforts at state-formation that characterized the Church and several kingdoms—England and France, Denmark, Poland and Hungary—in the eleventh and twelfth centuries.[3] These institutions attempted to define increasingly clearly, and to enforce the rules of what a Christian should believe and how Christians should live. As they did so the beliefs and practices of those who did not conform became more sharply defined and visible: those who chose not to adhere, "heretics"; and those whose beliefs and practices placed them outside the circle of Christian life, Jews and Muslims.

While this historic project depended on the action of positive identification, through beliefs captured and enacted in rituals, identity was also formed through shared fears and anxieties. Zones of purity and pollution, of comfort and of danger, were delineated within European places, physical as well as mental. Complex configurations of space, word and sound were created as representations and performances of the central Christian tenets: Incarnation and Redemption, intercession through the Virgin Mary, collective membership in the Church. Cathedrals in cities did this most effectively and impressively, but each parish church was a version of the integrated vision, which Christians were taught to imagine. There were sacraments as channels of grace, priests as ritual actors, liturgical action as an occasion for re-enactment of sacred history, and prayer as a cry for hope and consolation.

This holistic vision is made vivid in a sermon—though it may never have been delivered—by an unknown yet highly impressive preacher, for an audience at Amiens cathedral some time in 1269. The Cathedral's west façade, with its three portals, echoes the sermon in proclaiming the possibilities offered to humanity: the blend of good works, ecclesiastical provision, and the loving intercession of the Virgin Mary. (Figure 1.) The preacher wrote his sermon in French; he deployed none of the conventional rhetorical structures which characterized learned sermons of his day. His was a more discursive, less formal, yet highly appealing style, which balanced effectively the sense of sin and the hope for salvation.[4]

The west façade and the sermon combine well into a world view and a way of life. Both integrate idea and matter, are at once universal and very local. The cathedral was still being built when the sermon was written, and had it been delivered it would have been in a church as yet incomplete. At the heart of Amiens, a center of commerce and administration, the preacher did not shy from mentioning the fundamental reckoning, the "accounting" that bound believers and their church:

> What they do for the sweet Mother of God, Saint Mary, will not go unrewarded. Now, take a good look at yourselves, at whether you have observed the feast days prescribed for the past year.
>
> May God help me! I think there is much to amend.
>
> Afterwards you will have won something worth even more, for by simply coming to church from home, they accrue forty days of true pardon, without giving a penny or halfpenny, and forty days true pardon for meeting the needs of the [church of the] sweet Mother of God, Saint Mary, that she [or it] be fulfilled [or completed].[5]

The preacher is practical in his guidance to the audience, as he spells out the meaning of human transgression within the sacred economy. From discussing lust he moves to the penalties for abusing the marriage vows:

> For you should know that whoever destroys and breaks up marriage tears up and destroys the good flesh of our Lord; he denies the holy sacrament; he violates the holy scripture and the holy words of our Lord. [6]

In the cathedral dedicated to Mary—that most universal of saints—there was none the less a strong awareness of locality, and the preacher enhanced it with detail. The lives of Christians in Amiens diocese were served by 777 priests; it was home to twenty-six abbeys headed by twenty-six abbots. All these were hard at work, celebrating masses, doing good works, providing charity and relief.[7] The diocese was a sort of machine, with many cogs of differentiated action, which together produced the incessant functioning of a Christian society. There is an earthiness, a reassuring familiarity in the words and the matter, and no doubt the music and sound which were produced in Amiens Cathedral for thousands to hear and see on feast days. This was a celebration of the modular formula which marked European religious cultures: a universal system for the dispensation of grace, the sacraments, mediated by the clergy—inspired and sometimes supported by other religious, especially friars. All this was experienced through local articulations: language, music, building stone, organization of space, local saints, even local versions of Mary. Here was a formula of great potency and malleability, and the man who wrote the sermon for Amiens was fully aware of its potential. One can imagine such preaching on occasion in all European cities and towns, at courts, and at pilgrimage shrines. These were not routine events, but they marked the incursion of charisma—the preacher's unique gift—into the lives of its audience; they provided a vivid image of a Christian world and the believer's place within it.

* * *

How might we imagine the presence of non-Christians in cities so strongly, indelibly and copiously marked by Christian images, time and sounds? [8]

Jews were central to the telling of the core narratives of Christianity. They were present as actors in biblical tale, in miracles stories, and in accounts of more recent enormities: ritual murder, blasphemy, host desecration, abuse of images. The cultural process which made Christianity so vivid, accessible and relevant to people's lives, also made the Jew increasingly present and active. For the devotional world that respected Mary and approached the Passion through Mary's eyes, also placed emphasis on the role of the Jews: their agency, their guilt.[9]

The thirteenth century saw the movement into the vernacular and the diversification of genres used for the discussion and dissemination of religious matter. It had been preceded by almost two centuries of scholastic debate in schools and universities, where Christian theology and law were codified and discussed in scholastic method. Those who considered and expressed the central tenets in *summae* and specialized tracts, also turned on occasion to polemic as a method of intellectual debate. Anselm of Canterbury, for example, provided some of the most compelling arguments for the Incarnation and Mary's role in it; he also wrote an imagined debate with a Jew. Odo of Tournai, Bishop of Cambrai (d. 1113), similarly wrote around 1100 a tract on Original Sin and the necessity of the Incarnation, as well as a debate with a Jew, Leo.[10]

Theological argument was mixed with invective, as in the following section, about Mary's purity, rejected and derided by the imagined Jews:

> *Odo*: ...Gabriel said that she is "full of grace." Therefore her sex was filled with glory, her womb was filled with glory, her organs were filled with glory, the whole of her was filled with glory....Where is that which you call the uncleanliness of woman, the obscene prison, the fetid womb? Confess you wretch your stupidity...[11]

Many writers active in the Anglo-French realm contributed to the genre *adversus iudaeos*: Anselm of Canterbury, Gilbert Crispin, Guibert of Nogent, Odo of Tournai, and more.[12] These writings arose from the milieu of monastic liturgy and biblical exegesis, it was bound up with the oppositional tropes of *ecclesia/synagoga, vetus/novus* and with the polemical affirmation of the truth of the Incarnation and the appropriation of the Bible as a collection of Christian proof-texts. Within the liturgy and its interpretation, in the drama enacted in cathedrals and monasteries, in the art of illumination, on objects that decorated altars, and on stone façades triumphant *ecclesia* emerged with power and promise.

These preoccupations touched the lives of those few involved in the interpretations of the biblical stories—monks, and those who parsed the biblical texts—scholars. Only rarely, though spectacularly, did charisma energize public massacres against Jews, where law failed to protect them, as the servants of kings, emperors and lords. The crusade massacres of 1096 and 1145, the narrative invention of ritual murder which took place in Norwich in the 1150s, were each a unique testing of routines which for the most part kept the peace, the peculiar life routines of Jewish residents in European towns and cities, a people unto themselves in so many ways.[13] The monastic chroniclers who describe the events from the Christian point of view are often shockingly poisonous.[14] We have little access to the points of view of the people among whom Jews lived, nothing to set alongside the monastic accounts.

By the thirteenth century a great deal had happened to move the center of cultural production into the vernacular. Whole cohorts of writers, preachers, artists and poets now filled the ranks of the professional mediators in towns and cities, in courts and in villages too. Monks were early translators, like the French Benedictine monk and abbot, Gautier de Coinci (1177– 1236), who not only composed words and music in praise of Mary, but also translated tales of her miracles from Latin to French. In a world which was becoming ever fuller of knowledge of Mary and even more familiar with representations of her, he chose to expound Mary-lore while dwelling on the ever-present danger posed to her by the Jews. Gautier's praise of Mary is clear and confident:

> Fresh and bright rose,
> full of the Holy Spirit,
> you will be daughter and mother
> to the sovereign son of God.
> Your substance was so very
> orderly, pure and harmonious
> that in you your father took
> human form and flesh.
>
> Lady, who is so holy
> and who was so chosen
> who was made great with child
> by the Holy Spirit,
> listen to my petition
> and turn yourself towards me.[15]

In these decades during which Mary became a common feature of most parish churches, of cathedral façades, of public spaces and even of domestic interiors, it was easy to imagine not only daily contact with her—kneeling to a statue, reciting the Ave Maria, habitual and short prayer—but also occasional attacks by Mary's perceived "enemies." A story, which had spread from Constantinople since at least the seventh century, was rewritten by Gautier into a miraculous narrative for his own time. The Jew in question was "malicious and nasty, who despised Christianity greatly" (lines 12-13); while he visited a Christian's house he looked through a window

> .... and saw a panel
> On which an image was painted
> In the likeness of Our Lady.
> Feigning ignorance:
> "Tell me," he said, "tell me please,
> Of whom is this image?"
> "It is," he said, "of the maiden
> Who was so pure, serene and clean
> That the lord of the whole world
> Took humanity within her body."[16]

The Jew proceeded to taunt the Christian and to deride the veneration of Mary; to show just how he felt he finally threw the panel into a privy. The

Christian was moved to an act of pious restoration, once he recovered from the shock:

> He ran to the privy,
> To seek the image, and found it there.
> He proved himself to be a decent man:
> He washed it and cleaned it,
> Repaired and restored it
> So it was even more beautiful than before.[17]

The image was indeed now better still, since from it poured miraculous oil. This oil benefited only those who loved Mary; those, like the Jew, who did not, could not enjoy its sweet—"douce"—effect.

Gautier de Coinci worked by intuition to express a growing unease with the Jewish presence in medieval towns. The dramas of separation which ultimately dislodged Jews—their fruitful contributions, their lively communities—from nearly all European urban centers by the later Middle Ages, were as yet only experimental in nature and sporadic. As the urban space became the hub of the creative, "modern" meeting of commerce, administration, learning and the privileges of the court, it was also the home of most—though not all—Jews.[18]

Urban spaces were the setting in which many of Mary's miraculous incursions into Christian lives were imagined, and these interventions were often punitive acts against the Jews, her enemies. So formative to the making of the Christian polity did such narratives become that a collection of Marian tales was conceived in the court of a very Christian king. The *Cantigas de Santa Maria* is the collection of 429 Marian miracles, collected under the patronage of King Alfonso X, the Wise, of Castile, in the 1260s. This king aimed to weave his disparate domains, among them regions and peoples recently brought into the Christian sphere through "reconquest"; he strove to produce a Christian ethic in law, ritual and religious culture. The *Cantigas de Santa Maria* were produced in lavish—some illuminated—manuscripts, some with musical notation for performance at court and beyond. They formed a collection of old and new Marian tales, stories which haled from shrines and communities throughout the Christian world, the vast majority of which are Iberian, local. These were reworked into verse, each a narrative accompanied by a moralizing refrain.

Such is the story of Mary and the Jews of Toledo: on the feast of the Assumption, while the Archbishop of Toledo celebrated the mass, a woman began weeping:

> Oh, God, oh, God, how great and manifest is the perfidy of the Jews, who killed my Son, though they were His own people, and even now they wish no peace with him.
>
> After the mass the archbishop recounted and interpreted the event: clearly the Jews were enacting an evil deed:
> Then they all hastily set out for the Jewish quarter and found, it is no lie, an image of Jesus Christ, which the Jews were striking and spitting upon.
> And furthermore, the Jews had made a cross upon which they intended to hang the image. For this deed they were all to die, and their pleasure was turned to grief.
> *Refrain: What most offends Holy Mary is a wrong done to Her Son.*[19]

Jews who lived in Christian communities clearly knew a great deal about Christian life and enjoyed some access to sacred symbols and spaces. By the thirteenth century contact between Jews and such important markers of Christian identity was freighted with suspicion of evil intent. Narratives available within the religious culture increasingly attributed to Jews blasphemous purpose and evil conspiracy; this turned neighborhoods into a menace not only a source of familiar and comfortable interaction. Yet some of the poems of the *Cantigas de Santa Maria* also imagined a different type of neighborliness, one which was conducive to conversion, in several miracle tales about Muslims. So, for example, when a Muslim woman took a child in her care, who had died of a terrible disease, to the Virgin of Salas (a shrine in the diocese of Zaragoza), Mary affected a cure. The Muslim woman acted as she had seen Christians act, and to the disapproval of her own friends:

> "For I shall take my son to Holy Mary of Salas right away, with this waxen image which I have bought for her. I shall keep watch in the church of the most blessed Holy Mary, and I believe that she will sympathize with my woe."
> She did just that and indeed the child was brought back to life. She converted "for she saw that Holy Mary had given him back to her alive, and she always held Her in great reverence."
> *Refrain: The Virgin will aid whoever trusts in her and prays faithfully to Her, although he be a follower of another law.*[20]

The figure of Mary offered an occasion to dwell on Christian identity in a particularly pointed way within a society where Jews and Muslims were familiar neighbors. The Iberian Marian tales invoked the sense of a Christian geography which transcended the boundaries of kingdoms. They tell of familiar and much loved shrines which drew pilgrims and kept them enthralled for life with memories and eruptions of the miraculous. All these were brought together by a ruler whose image portrayed piety, benign care but also a crusader's commitment to "liberating" Christian lands. The *Cantigas* offered possibilities for personal devotion, communal celebration and collective sharing, as well as a vision of a Christian state.

* * *

In the Italian cities of the same period a different political settlement—a civic dispensation—encouraged a wide range of local initiatives and broad participation in public life and religious display. In one region a particular devotional and ethical style developed, soon to affect the whole of Europe. It was inspired by the example of the charismatic Francis of Assisi, the *alter christus*. The devotional style was one of performance in the streets, group devotion, all in memory of Christ. Attention was drawn to the humanity of the suffering Christ, to the memory and mimesis of that legacy, here and now. It is not surprising that new artistic forms were also created there to capture that style: large crucifixes adorned Tuscan churches, overhanging the viewer for the most direct of gazes (Figure 2). There was a particular style in depiction of mourning, which involved the whole body, as displayed in Giotto's art (Figure 3).

And there was more. For Franciscan friars led lay people to enact the Passion in new and audacious ways. In confraternities created by urban lay people, men as well as women, new techniques of performance and imitation were developed. People enacted the Passion, as we will see at greater length in Chapter 3, through rhythmic recitation of verses in their dialect, accompanied by gestures of flagellation, mortification, and sometimes in communal song. This context made the Jew a cruel inflictor of pain, an actor in the great drama of salvation. A verse chanted by the members of a flagellant company in fourteenth-century Modena began with the refrain:

> Woe to me, Jews, cruel people.
> How embittered must your heart be,
> That you have crucified
> Jesus Christ the all powerful?[21]

And then turns to nature, for evidence of Jewish misdeed:

> Look at the sun, who for sorrow
> has removed its splendor,
> it cannot bear to see such harshness
> towards Christ its creator.
>
> And the earth suffering
> is all atremble for pain
> because of your great mistake
> which you have demonstrated in this.[22]

It ends with a cry to Jews and other sinners:

> O Jews, and all people,
> who live in mortal sin,
> if you believed, you would
> do that which Christ had ordained
> and truly admit
> of all your sin
> then you will receive from all powerful God
> the reign which he has made for the world.[23]

The powerful vision which originated in central Italy and was carried and animated by friars, spread to a wide range of European spheres and groups. A devotional genre which depicted Mary's lament in verse was accessible by the second half of the thirteenth century in many languages and registers. A manuscript made by three Hungarian friars, probably Dominicans, rendered into their mother tongue something of the immediacy of the chants which they had learned during their sojourn in Italy. Its eight stanzas are each four verses long, and most are two words short. Christ is addressed as "World of world/ flower of flowers"; he is Mary's "Jewish son." There is frequent mention of sweetness and honey, of the shedding of Jesus's blood and Mary's tears. A second lament, four stanzas long, describes the detail of the Crucifixion at the hand of lawless Jews, a Passion in which Mary wished to join her son. The Hungarian preachers absorbed and conveyed the mood, style and context of Italian vernacular chants of Mary's Passion.[24]

The encounters of Mary and the Jews were increasingly associated with the remembered narratives, vernacular chants and the images seen time and again in churches and on public buildings. While scholars and religious leaders sometimes debated the Incarnation and Virgin Birth in the course of staged disputations, there were more mundane encounters of varying degrees of intensity in city streets and on the routes of pilgrimage and trade.[25] As Mary became more visible in streets and squares, so did the possibilities for unfortunate clashes between Christians and Jews around her. By the fifteenth century Mary inhabited many a street-corner, becoming a constant reminder to Christians of the conventions of Christian life.[26] Authorities attempted to regulate the public space and avoid conflict, and so in fifteenth-century Mantua, for example, there was a procedure whereby a Jew might remove a religious image when he purchased a house decorated with one. Yet moments of excitement and agitation, moments in which enthusiasm and charisma affected people's lives, sometimes heightened the stakes beyond the routines foreseen by officials. When this occurred in Mantua in 1495 a Jew was refused the permission to remove an image of Mary and Child on its front because of the intervention of the urban crowd. What is more, Daniele da Norsa was required to pay for a new painting which came to be known as the Madonna of Victory, by the local painter, destined to fame, Andrea Mantegna. The growing ubiquity of Mary contributed to the possibilities of mobilization around images and processions in the public domain; it encouraged performances of identity occasioned by Mary's presence.[27]

Mary could endow a space with identity, and one which was particularly poignant as a statement against Jews. In the course of the fifteenth century urban politics of several German cities led to expulsions of their Jewish communities, often prompted by the lobbying of guilds and facilitated by the preaching of friars. The spaces left empty in the heart of cities offered opportunities: properties were reallocated, stones were used for the erection of new buildings, and synagogues were sometimes turned into Marian chapels.[28] Soon after the *Reichstadt* Regensburg was allowed by the Emperor (after years of pleading) to expel its Jews in 1518, a miracle narrative linked the space with the Virgin Mary. It involved a laborer who was wounded in the course of clearing the site and cured through Mary's intervention in response to his wife's prayers. The miracle was identified and all proper procedures followed: a chapel was built on the site, a booklet described the miracles, and indulgences were granted to visitors.[29] Above all, through Mary Regensburg was redefined as a city free of Jews, as a community blessed by Mary's care, and as part of the holy geography of shrine and pilgrimage. The statue made for the site was of the type which we will discuss in the next chapter—the *schöne Maria*—Mary and her child: sweet, loving and beautiful (Figure 4).

The imaginary repertoire which linked Jews, heretics and blasphemers with wanton destruction of Marian imagery was revived in the course of the sixteenth century in those communities which saw religious strife between Christians. The power of the abused image is as manifest as it had been to the audience of Gautier de Coinci's tale more than three hundred years earlier. And so, for example, on a night in Easter week 1533 in Tournai, when a debauched character attacked a prostitute she turned for help to an image of the Virgin on the Gate of Saint-Fontaine from which he had entered. The attacker derided her: "you are indeed mad if you believe that she will help you, because she has no power and she is as much a virgin as you, a common prostitute, are."[30] On the morrow the figure was found to be bleeding, and by Holy Friday it was removed and carried to the church of Mary Magdalene, where it was treated like a reliquary ("digne reliquaire"). The great and the good—clergy and civic dignitaries alike—visited the image, and in less than fortnight a general procession was ordered with a sermon on God and the Virgin Mary.[31]

* * *

Mary became in the later medieval centuries a test of Christian identity, a hurdle for membership and part of the *habitus* of Christian life. Two powerful images developed around her: the young mother with her baby son, and the grieving mother witness to her grown son's suffering and death. Emotional habits, and maybe even emotional communities, developed around these images. The affinities nurtured by families in their homes combined with the possibilities offered by a vibrant public religious culture to endow Europeans with a sentimental education, and with a repertoire of identities for life.

Notes

[1] Natalie Z. Davis, "The Rites of Violence," in *Society and Culture in Early Modern France: Eight Essays*, London, 1975, pp. 152–87; first published in *Past and Present* 59 (1973), pp. 51–91.
[2] Miri Rubin, "Identities," in *A Social History of England, 1200–1500*, ed. Rosemary Horrox and Mark Ormrod, Cambridge, 2006, pp. 383–412.
[3] R. I. Moore, *The Formation of a Persecuting Society: Authority and Deviance in Western Europe 950–1250*, second edn., Oxford, 2007. This edition includes comments by the author in response to the reception of the first edition, published in 1987, with the subtitle *Power and Deviance in Western Europe, 950–1250*.
[4] For a summary of the sermon and its moral message see Stephen Murray, *A Gothic Sermon: Making a Contract with the Mother of God, Saint Mary of Amiens*, Berkeley (CA), 2004, pp. 13–25.
[5] "Ce n'est pas corvée qu'il feront à la douce mere diu sainte Marie; or prenés garde entre vous, se vous avés bien gardées les festes, que vous a commandées tout l'an contreval.
Si m'aït dex! Ge cuit qu'il i a moult à amender.
Après i gaaigniés vous encore qui mex vaut, que pour seulement venir de leurs maisons au mostier, il gaaignent XL iornées de vrai pardon, sans doner denier ne obole, et XL iornées de vrai pardon, pour atendre le besoigne le douce mere diu sainte Marie que ele soit aconsomée," *Ibid*, pp. 70–71. On the city and its economy see Stephen Murray, *Notre-Dame Cathedral of Amiens: the Power of Change in Gothic*, Cambridge, 1996, pp. 19–27.
[6] "Car sachiés vraiement quiconques depieche ne deront mariage il deront et depiece la bele char nostre segneur, il desment le saint sacrament nostre segneur, il desdit et deffait la sainte escriture et le saintes paroles nostre segneur," Murray, *A Gothic Sermon*, pp. 92–3.

[7] *Ibid*, pp. 114–15. For an insight into the life of Amiens cathedral canons see Page, *The Owl and the Nightingale: Musical Life and Ideas in France 1100–1300*, London, 1989, p. 136.

[8] Amiens was, in fact, one of the few northern French towns which excluded Jewish migration from the mid-twelfth century, William Chester Jordan, *The French Monarchy and the Jews: From Philip Augustus to the Last Capetians*, Philadelphia (PA), 1989, pp. 34, 155 and map on p. 156.

[9] A unique and luxurious artifact which exemplifies this vision is the *Bible moralisée*, studied in Sara Lipton, *Images of Intolerance: the Representation of Jews and Judaism in the Bible moralisée*, Berkeley (CA), 1999.

[10] Odo of Tournai, *On Original Sin; and, A Disputation with the Jew, Leo, concerning the Advent of Christ, the Son of God: Two Theological Treatises*, trans. Irven M. Resnick, Philadelphia (PA), 1994.

[11] *Ibid*, pp. 79–80.

[12] On this period and its writings see Anna Sapir Abulafia, *Christians and Jews in the Twelfth-Century Renaissance*, London, 1995.

[13] Jonathan Elukin, *Living Together, Living Apart*, Princeton (NJ), 2007.

[14] See, for example, the making of the myth of ritual murder by a monk of Norwich Cathedral Priory in Simon Yarrow, *Saints and their Communities: Miracle Stories in Twelfth Century England*, Oxford, 2006, chapter 5, especially pp. 123–40.

[15] Rose fresche et clere
   Dou Saint Espir plainne,
   Tu iez fille et mere
   Au fil Dieu demaine.

Tant fu ta matere
Nete et pure et sainne
Qu'en toi prist tes pere
Char et forme humainne.
Dame, qui tant sainte
Et qui tant fu eslite
Que grose et enchainte
Fus dou Saint Esperite,
Oiez ma complainte
Et envers moi t'apite,

Gautier de Coinci, *Les miracles de Nostre Dame* I, ed. V. Frederic Koenig, Geneva and Lille, 1955, III, p. 35, lines 73–86.

[16] ... et vit una tavlete
Ou painte avoit une ymagete
A la semblance Nostre Dame.
"Di moi, fait il, di moi, par t'ame,
Ceste ymage de cui est ele?
-Ele est, fait il, de la pucele
Qui tant fu pure, nete et monde
Que li sires de tot le monde
Humanité prist en ses flans

Gautier de Coinci, *Les miracles de Nostre Dame* II, ed. V. Frederic Koenig, Geneva and Paris, 1961, pp. 101–104, lines 17–25.

[17] A la privee corant vint,
L'image quist, si la trova.
Com loiax hom bien se prova:
Lavee l'a et netoïe,
Si l'a remise et retirie,
Plus belement que n'ert devant,

Ibid, p. 103, lines 58–63.

[18] Robin R. Mundill, *England's Jewish Solution: Experiment and Expulsion, 1262–1290*, Cambridge, 1998, has contributed a great deal to acquaintance with Jewish presence in small towns and rural communities.

[19] *Songs of Holy Mary of Alfonso X, The Wise: a Translation of the Cantigas de Santa Maria*, trans. Kathleen Kulp-Hill, Tempe (AZ), 2000, no. 12, p. 19:

> E a voz, come chorando,/ dizia: 'Ay Deus, ai Deus,
> com' é mui grand' e provada/ a perfia dos judeus
> que meu Fillo mataron, seendo seus,
> e aynda non queren conosco paz.'
> *O que a Santa Maria mais despraz,*
> *é de quen ao seu Fillo pesar faz;*
>
> Enton todos mui correndo/ começaron logo d'ir
> dereit' aa judaria,/ e acharon, sen mentir,
> omagen de Jeso-Crist', a que ferir
> yan os judeus e cospir-lle ne faz.
> *O que a Santa Maria mais despraz,*
> *é de quen ao seu Fillo pesar faz;*
>
> E sen aquesta', os judeus/ fezeran ũa cruz fazer
> en que aquela omagen/ querian logo põer.
> E por est' ouveron todos de morrer,
> e tornou-e-lles en doo seu solaz.
> *O que a Santa Maria mais despraz,*
> *Ée de quen ao seu Fillo pesar faz,*

Cantigas de Santa Maria I, ed. Walter Mettmann, Coimbra, 1959, no. 12, pp. 88-9, lines 16-20, 26-35.

[20] *Songs of the Holy Mary*, no. 167, p. 202;
   Ca eu levarei meu fillo/ a Salas desta vegada
   con ssa omagen de cera/ que ja lle tenno comprada,
   e velarei na eigreja/ da mui benaventurada
   Santa Maria, e tenno/ que de mia coita se sença;
   e tornou logo crischãa/ pois viu que llo vivo dera
   Santa Maria, e sempre/ a ouv' en gran reverença,
Cantigas de Santa Maria II, Coimbra, 1961, no. 167, pp. 170–1; lines 20-24, 37-8.
[21] Oymè, Çudei, la crudelle çente,
   Como lo coro vostro è açegato,
   Che Jeso Cristo omnipotente
   Aviti sì crucifigato?
Il laudario dei Battuti de Modena, ed. Giulio Bertoni, Halle, 1909, XL, p. 46, lines 1–4 and later as refrain.
[22] Vidi lo sole chi per tristeça
   À retrato lo so'splendore,
   Ch' el non veça tanta aspreça
   In Cristo so' criatore.

   E la terra per grameça
   Trema tuta per dolore
   Del vostro grande errore
   Chi avi inço' monstrato,
Ibid, lines 5–12.
[23] O çudei, e tuta çente,
   Chi si in mortale peccato,
   Se crederiti, fariti
   Quello che Cristo à ordenato
   E inserire veraxemente

> D'ugni uostro peccato
> Averiti da deo omnipotente
> Lo regno chi per lo mundo è facto,

Ibid, p. 47, lines 48–55.

[24] Robert Gragger, "Eine altungarische Marienklage," in *Ungarische Bibliothek* 7, Berlin and Leipzig, 1923, pp. 1–21; at pp. 18–9.

[25] On Mary and disputations see William Chester Jordan, "Marian Devotion and the Talmud Trial of 1240," in *Religionsgespräche im Mittelalter*, ed. Bernard Lewis and Friedrich Niewöhner, Wolfenbütteler Mittelalter-Studien 4, Wiesbaden, 1992, pp. 61–76.

[26] Ed Muir, "The Virgin on the Street Corner: The Place of the Sacred in Italian Cities," in *Religion and Culture in the Renaissance and Reformation*, ed. Steven Ozment, Kirksville (MI), 1987, pp. 24–40.

[27] Michele Luzzati, "Ebrei, chiesa locale, 'principe' e popolo: due episodi di distruzione di immagini sacre alla fine del Quattrocento," in *La casa dell'ebreo: Saggi sugli Ebrei a Pisa e in Roscana nel Medioevo e nel Rinascimento*, Pisa, 1985, pp. 205–34; Dana E. Katz, "Painting and the Politics of Persecution: Representing the Jew in Fifteenth-Century Mantua," *Art History* 23 (2000), pp. 475–95.

[28] Hedwig Röckelein, "Marie, l'église et la synagogue: culte de la Vierge et lutte contre les Juifs en Allemagne à la fin du Moyen-Âge," in *Marie: le culte de la vierge dans la société médiévale*, Paris, 1996, pp. 512–32; see also Mary Minty, "*Judengasse* to Christian Quarter: The Phenomenon of the Converted Synagogue in the Late Medieval and Early Modern Holy Roman Empire," in *Popular Religion in Germany and Central Europe, 1400–1800*, Basingstoke, 1996, pp. 58–86.

[29] Philip M. Soergel, *Wondrous in his Saints: Counter-Reformation Propaganda in Bavaria*, Berkeley (CA), 1993, pp. 53–5.
[30] 'Tu es bien folle si tu cuyde quelle te ayde, car elle na nulle puissance et quelle est vierge autant que toy qui es putain publicque,' Olivier Christin, *Une révolution symbolique: l'iconoclasme Huguenot et la reconstruction catholique*, Paris, 1991, p. 179.
[31] On retouching of images see Cathleen Hoeniger, *The Renovation of Paintings in Tuscany, 1250–1500*, Cambridge, 1995.

Chapter 3

Emotions and Selves

Following the footsteps of Natalie Zemon Davis, and very much in her honor, the previous two chapters traced the possibilities of a global history and the creation of terrains of polemic and encounter within the vast and important culture field that developed around Mary in medieval Europe.

In this chapter we will continue the enterprise of identifying Tasks and Themes in the Study of European Culture, by studying the emergence of a European style of emotive devotion. For in the centuries that followed the year one thousand, the Mary of prayer, the lady of intercession, became increasingly an enabling site for reflection on the expression of emotion. It began with the exploration of the happy motherhood of birth and nurture, and later also came to encompass the tragic motherhood of loss and mourning. I suggest that these images—the tender mother and child, the tragic *pietà*—produced in medieval Europe and later spread the world wide are still part of a European language of affect, part of what may make Europeans at some moments into an emotional community.

I use the term emotional community, recently developed by the American scholar Barbara Rosenwein, in the book of 2006 which carries that name. She defines such a community as "groups in which people adhere to the same notions of emotional expression and value—or devalue—the same or related emotions." This idea suggests something like the discursive frame of Foucault, and even more the *habitus* of Bourdieu, that is a frame of action and reflection which also privileges the body and its habits, space of performance and interaction between individuals. Rosenwein builds much on the work of Martha Nussbaum who talks of emotion as an "upheaval of thought" common to all people, deeply engrained in the mind. Rosenwein emphasizes more than Nussbaum does the cultural specificity of the articulation of emotion—which according to the Oxford English Dictionary describes "joy, love, anger, fear, happiness, guilt, sadness, embarrassment, hope." It is a word that has only appeared quite recently in Anglophone usage, replacing the word Passion. She dismisses the evolutionary frame offered by Norbert Elias, who has had a great renaissance of late, and identifies variety in the practices of early medieval Europe—her own scholarly terrain—between many different frames of emotional propriety that defy a single diachronic progression.

How can we know about emotions? How can we touch the private and the personal, how can we reach it within the public and collective spheres? Medieval historians do not expect to come across revealing ego-documents, though some noted autobiographies have survived, and other genres were also used—poetry, devotional writing—to convey explicit reflections on the self. When using such sources we must be attuned to the influence of genre and rhetoric, two associated resources available to educate people. It is also useful to think of ways in which people could express their identity and feelings in public and shared sphere: devotional behavior and comportment offered a whole array of prompts and opportunities for expression.

Devotional images are resources which offered identifications, somewhat specular—prompting the question "could that be me?"—directive, alluring, and for us abundant. Images of Mary were particularly rich in offering opportunities for identification. So much of what was said of Mary, even more than is the case with her son, was expressed in the language of *mimesis,* an emotional register of communication. Example, imitation, and compassion were the emotional lessons taught by devotional writings. Moments for reflection on motherhood, conjugality, virginity, nurture, and bereavement, were all offered up around the well-known and loved figure of Mary.

* * *

The centers of discussion and production of ideas, rituals and artifacts related to Mary were monastic houses that maintained elaborate systems of liturgy and prayer. Monks and nuns devoted to the struggle against sin and immersion in devotional work were particularly aware of the precarious balance between human striving and human frailty. The eleventh and twelfth centuries saw the development of ideas and practices that offered believers avenues for penance and atonement. The idea of purgatory matured in the twelfth century; it became a place where believers suffered for minor sins after death, and for a limited period of time. Purgatory offered hope, but also the knowledge of pain, for all but the saints and the damned were expected to spend a period of purgation, cleansing, suffering in the middle place. In all these operations some consolation alleviated the occasional despair. The figure of Mary was a particularly efficacious companion; she could console but also act with miraculous interventions and intercession with her son.

We are best informed about the emotional worlds of monks and nuns in these centuries, lives that followed the rhythms of a rule, but were never fully circumscribed by it. Religious houses—and cathedrals within the hubbub of big cities—maintained unceasing routines of prayer, a blend of personal petitions within a collective liturgical format. As monks and nuns repeatedly intoned their psalms and the prayers at the daily mass, on feast days at commemoration of benefactors, they also developed a personal style of expression in prayer. We learn about such prayer from the compositions of renowned devotional poets—around 1100 the prayers composed by Anselm of Lucca and Anselm of Canterbury were subsequently requested, copied and cherished—and from the activities of composition and copying which routinely took place in religious houses.[1] The prayers that drew so much favor were usually meditative in tone; they tended towards introspection and self-abasement. The illustrations which accompanied prayers within psalters sometimes capture the moment of adoration/prostration, like that of the nun adoring Christ in the Psalter of the nunnery at Shaftesbury, whose abbess Eulalia enjoyed a friendship with Anselm of Canterbury.[2]

As the religious explored their inner selves and aimed to distance themselves from sin, Mary emerged as their companion. The struggle was a hard one, and in it Mary was frequently and increasingly chosen as a specialy friend. Her humanity was without doubt, and so was her unique affinity to the celestial realm, and to the source of all grace, her son. In monasteries and in some cathedral schools Europe's theological settlement was being refined and disseminated further. In the conception of the Christian order there was increased emphasis on the necessity of the Incarnation, and of Mary's role in bringing it about. Mary was increasingly and more passionately than before invoked in the prayers of monks and nuns, to whose search for consolation was added the sense of Mary's unique powers to mentor and assist. Within monasteries, prayers and invocations were composed, and these were disseminated widely to interested and exalted lay people, to cathedrals and to priories.

This figure of Mary was one of justice and wisdom and maternal presence. The twelfth-century glass of Chartres Cathedral, that seat of one of Europe's foremost schools, presented Mary as a crowned and jeweled woman, clad in blue, enthroned and facing the viewer, with her son in her lap.[3] This is the figure of Mary as Seat of Wisdom, whose origins are in the imperial rendering of the Theotokos (Figure 5). By the twelfth century it was to be seen in the loftiest of choirs, like the gilt silver bejeweled Virgin and Child in Toledo Cathedral; by the early thirteenth also in the most modest of parishes.[4]

Marian lyrics and prayers, as well as visual representations, like the wooden statues so common in French parish churches, became available to lay people in local idioms and in familiar settings in the course of the late-twelfth and thirteenth centuries. The move to the spoken language meant that a wide range of genres was now used to discuss Mary. Every genre was linked to a set of social practices: works for teaching the people of the parish, poetry for the use of religious confraternities, guidebooks for pilgrims, collections of miracles in the vernacular, hymns and chanted prayers. Mary took on increasingly the colors of daily life; she dwelt within surroundings familiar to most people.

The cultural shift that saw the re-making of Mary in the "mother" tongue inserted her into webs of identity and emotion that became part of the European experience for the many. Mary's figure was unique since she was at once understood as a human but was also privileged with purity and virtue and the powers to act miraculously in the world. It was the exploration of Mary's humanity which attracted most attention, and which inspired emotional responses, and this occurred above all when Mary was imagined as the mother of a tender child, or as the mother beholding the suffering of her grown son.

The traditional Mary of solemn statuesque presence was subtly being transformed in all media and many contexts of practice. The change rendered Mary a tender mother, engaged with her child. Mother and son were shown in touch and in play, smiling, gazing at each other and holding various object of natural beauty. From northern France spread a "Gothic" version of Mary and child in ivories and stone statues, and in them Mary stood with a child at her side, smiling, her body curved in an effort to balance the weight of her child (Figure 6).[5] The cultural sphere of England, and parts of Germany and the Low Countries absorbed these lessons, producing ever more playful emotion-laden figures of Mary. Frontal Mary was full of mystery and power, solid, erect, bearing memories of unknown majesty, eastern and ancient. The new Mary was young, tender and motherly.

The chronicler Matthew Paris was a sophisticated observer of European life in its many forms. Monk at the abbey of St Albans, he was familiar with the many genres of Mary lore, not least the traditions of miracle tales, so influentially collated a century earlier at his monastery by Abbot Anselm. His *Chronica majora* is illustrated by his own hand, and most impressive is a parchment leaf on which three images of Christ were drawn: Christ in his mother's arms, Christ head on the Cross, Christ's head in glory.[6] Mother and child are shown as intimates; their faces touch and they bear a real family resemblance. Like so many creative people of his time Paris sought to represent an emotional bond between Mary and her son, and this bond was an offering to be replicated in the relations of monk to Mary, and by extension of each and every Christian and Mary. By viewing and reflecting upon the love between mother and child, Europeans were encouraged to ponder a whole range of feelings and possibilities in their own religious practice. Mary was transformed over these decades from wise and majestic to tender and beautiful.

It was probably such a crowned Mary with a child in her womb the German poet Frauenlob (c. 1250–1318)—Henry of Meissen—one of the most original and startling poets of Mary, had in mind when he wrote:

> Listen! I saw a vision:
> a Lady on a throne.
> Great with child, that woman
> wore a wondrous crown.
>
> How she ached for the hour
> of birth, the best of women!
> In her crown of power
> I saw twelve gemstones glisten.[7]

Frauenlob delighted in the possibilities of a new intense emotional bond, which mirrored the physical closeness of mother and son. Rendered in courtly lyric this bond is unambiguously physical:

> How intimate he was with me
> locked in my little room!
> Who will lead me to the lily dell
> where my courtly lover hid so well?
> I am the high court's chamber

> where they heard the case of Eve's fall –
> I, the echo hall.
> Dear friends, remember:
> in the music of my dawn, I awake exalted song;
> from ancient night I bring the morn.[8]

From the figure of wisdom and majesty—so central to the practices centered on the struggle against sin and the rendering of self to judgement—Mary became in the vernaculars of Europe a contemporary child, adolescent, pregnant woman, wife, mother, neighbor, kinswoman; she was also imagined at work: cooking, feeding, spinning, and reading.

* * *

The cultural trend towards imitation—*mimesis*—meant not only identification with the suffering of Christ, martyrs and saints, but also the search for vestiges of the holy in the mundanity of human life.[9] Just as the enthroned Virgin became a vibrant figure of animated love, so the scene of the cross became a site of animated sadness. Quite like the transformation we just witnessed throughout the late twelfth and thirteenth centuries, that which produced the loving figure of mother and son, so it was with the scene of the Passion.

From a scene of decorous witness, with Mary and John the Evangelist either side of the crucified Christ, his body calm and majestic, against a background of gold, the Passion was being explored for the possibilities of humanization. This meant not only greater care in the representation of Christ's suffering body—always a balance between pain and abjection[10]—but also in the treatment of the witnesses, Mary and John. First with gentle hand gestures, then by the turning away of the head in pain, and ultimately, by the fourteenth century, with Mary utterly overcome by the sight.

It is not surprising that the culture of religious display which was fostered in cities encouraged imitation and invention: it was in the cities of central Italy that Francis of Assisi developed his unique religious style and in the cities of the Low Countries that the message found such strong echo. In cities and courts, where a variety of styles was supported by leisure, wealth and the activism of townspeople—men and women—the most creative blends of the personal and the public, the abject and the celebratory developed in late medieval religion.

The making of Mary familiar and vernacular was a long process in which friars engaged energetically. The world conjured in their preaching was produced from the dialectical movement between the lofty and the familiar, in human efforts to engage with the otherwordly. Hence, the central drama of salvation—the Passion—was retold through the eyes of a human; for highly privileged though Mary was she was but none the less human. Her witness, participation, suffering and imagined words attracted concerted literary, musical and visual efforts in the many genres of liturgy and drama, sermon and chant.

The most widely copied, translated and used tract of this type is the *Meditations on the Life of Christ*, probably composed by the Tuscan Franciscan, John of Caulibus, c. 1300, and until recently usually ascribed to St Bonaventure.[11] Here is a guide to Christ's life in 108 chapters, from cradle to grave. The chapters are based on biblical scenes, and at their heart is the Passion with many scenes leading up to it. The details of Christ's suffering are described by the author so as to conjure an image in the devotee's mind, as if she were a witness, like Christ's mother. The extent of elaboration is quite breathtaking, as the author himself admits in his account of the Passion based on Matthew 26:14–15: "It seems only right to tell not only of the penal and mortal crucifixion of the Lord, but also of those sufferings that were vehemently inflicted before it, of co-suffering, bitterness and stupor."[12] He then goes on to describe these acts of bitterness and torture in an abundance of detail animated by rhythmic repetition, in several short two-word phrases. Christ was given no rest in the lead-up to the Passion, all was struggle and conflict:

> One indeed seizes him;
> another binds him;
> another rises,
> yet another cries out;
> another pushes,
> another curses;
> another spits at him,
> another shakes him;
> another runs around in frenzy,
> another questions him;
> another seeks out false witnesses against him,
> another bands up with them;
> another bears false testimony against him,
> another accuses;
> another mocks,
> another blindfolds him;
> another turns his face,
> another boxes his ears;
> another leads him to the column,
> another arranges him on it;

> another hits him as he leads him,
> another pierces him,
> another shouts,
> another raises him up scornfully so as to shake him violently,
> another ties him to the column;
> another strikes him,
> another whips;
> another dressed him in purple in contempt,
> another crowned him with thorns;
> another puts a reed in his hand;
> another furiously raises him again so as to beat the head covered with thorns;
> another kneels in derision,
> and many others inflict [in this manner].[13]

The author addressed his audience, a Franciscan nun, with "listen and see," making her a privileged witness, like Mary, at the unfolding events. Like her, she should be compassionately linked to the events. Meditational chapters were offered for each Hour of the nun's day. It was a style of living, and of incessant feeling too, one intimately tied to Mary's imagined experience.

The vehicle for participation in Mary's suffering was a visual one: viewing images and imagining the graphic scenes which Mary experienced through her own vision. The visual was the powerful prompt for memorialization and reliving—the *imitatio*—of Mary's moment at the foot of the cross. English devotional poetry also emphasized Mary's gaze, as it imagined a dialogue between mother and son:

> "A son! Take heed to me whose son you were
> and set me up with you upon the cross
> For me here to leave, and you thus hence to go,
> is great care and woe to me.
> Cease now, Son, to be harsh to your mother,
> You who were always good to all others."
>
> "Stop now, Mother, and weep no more;
> your sorrow and your discomfort grieve me greatly.
> You know that in you I took human nature,
> in it to be afflicted, for the sake of human sin.
> Be now glad, Mother, and have in thought
> That human salvation, that I have sought, is now found.
> You shall not worry now about what you are to do,
> Lo! John, your kinsman, will be your son."[14]

The shared gaze and the shared feeling made the experience of the Crucifixion into a devotional experience mediated above all by Mary.

An extremely influential blending of styles and tastes—the static solemnity of Byzantine icons and the soft tones of French painting and sculpture—was achieved in Siena, a city which defined itself as Mary's own.[15] From the early thirteenth century local artists produced a local version of the highly influential Italo-Byzantine tradition: with much light, with warm skin tones, with highly decorative golden backgrounds. In Siena a European style developed, a combination of impulses towards delicate expressivity in figures who were still cast solemn and mournful. Mary was imagined as the solemn and majestic, as in the panel painting by the Master of Tressa for Siena Cathedral, the Madonna of the Large Eyes (*Madonna dagli occhi grossi*), in which her dark eyes are as penetrating as those shown on icons since the sixth century (Figure 7). Yet in the cathedral's crypt Mary appeared in her new, vernacular style: as a mother taking her son to school, in wall paintings that adorned the space where pilgrims assembled for instruction before their visit to the Duomo.[16] Mary was becoming at once increasingly visible in the decoration of churches, and a presence within domestic spaces, where private and family devotions were offered to her, a figure human and maternal.

The Sienese artist, Duccio di Buoninsegna (active by 1278–d. 1318) produced an image that captures much of this mood of tenderness around the figure of Mary and her Son. The small image, only 28 x 20.8 cm, was painted around 1295–1300, and was likely made for private devotional use. It is indeed extremely intimate, even when one sees it in the Metropolitan Museum of Art in New York (Figure 8).[17] Against a gold background and behind a painted parapet, Mary and child appear both highly traditional and dramatically new. Mary's large and solid body envelops the small, seemingly light, baby Jesus, who reaches gently towards his mother's face. Mary's fingers both hold and caress the boy, as he plays with her veil. She in blue, he in glorious purple and red, they gaze and contemplate each other. The faces are shaped into a family resemblance, echoed in the intimacy of touch. This trend continued; and by the end of the fourteenth century Mary and Child groups have very distinctive features, detailed clothes and a family resemblance. Giovanni Fei's (c. 1345–1411) panel in the great church from San Domenico in Siena, where the local saint Catherine of Siena habitually prayed, is an example of such bodily and familial closeness (Figure 9).[18]

Mary looks lovingly, but also sadly, at her son: Duccio's mother and child form a truly devotional image, which delights but also transports the viewer. On Mary's face mother love is apparent, but so is the foreknowledge of her child's end, the Passion, the focus of devotional practices in these cities. Images sometimes combined, in diptych form, the beginning and end, Mary and Child alongside the Man of Sorrows, Christ of the Passion. Mary attended at the beginning—birth and infancy, but also, and increasingly, at the end (Figure 10).

At the beginning of our period visual representations of the Crucifixion placed it against abstract, even empty backgrounds, with John the Evangelist standing to Christ's left and Mary to his right. Tuscan painted crucifixes were often accompanied by small figures of Mary and John either side of the middle of Jesus's body. Throughout the thirteenth century the tilting of the head or wringing of hands and anxious bending of fingers increasingly expressed emotions.[19] On the whole, Mary remained a figure of controlled sorrow, delicately symmetrical to that of John. But this balance was disrupted in the course of the thirteenth century as preaching and teaching of Jesus's life and death to Europeans of village and city parishes emphasized his quite human suffering on the cross, and his mother's subsequent agony. Scenes of the Crucifixion, now increasingly explored Mary's experience. Her body sometimes recoils, leans away from the cross, both hands are thrown into the air.[20] The tendency to dramatize Mary's suffering allowed her to be seen in some alarming new positions: fainting, leaning, falling, sometimes pulling at her son's body (Figure 11).

The process by which Mary was made local and familiar encouraged the exploration of emotion and empathy. Medieval adherents wondered how like them Mary really was. The leading cultural trend was towards an emphasis on empathy and this was enacted in lay associations, confraternities. The urban habits of consumption and display, of association and performance, enabled lay people to explore and participate in the imitation of God and his Mother even beyond the parish church. We have already appreciated the visual prompts of meditational seeing; the chants created for the use of confraternities encouraged a rhythmic discipline of sound, and the mobilization of the body into the whole which was devotional consideration of the Passion.

As we have seen in the preceding chapter confraternities were religious voluntary associations in which members explored devotional practices, commemorated the dead (and expected to be commemorated in turn), and joined people close to them in status and wealth in acts of charity and display. Here were devotional corporations with the collective power to act as patrons: they commissioned chants, music, drama, and art. Scores of such groups were recognized in big cities, and they were invited to participate in their livery in civic processions and contribute to the embellishment of the cityscape. Confraternities maintained chapels, invited preachers, commissioned altarpieces and processed. They acted privately as well as publicly, and offered a setting that was safe and familiar for enactment of devotion and the performance of extravagant emotion. The commonest themes were penitent flagellation, commemoration of the Crucifixion, and the praise of Mary.

The principle of *mimesis*, which we have already encountered, combined the memory of suffering and the outpouring of praise. It was the very suffering of Mary that was praiseworthy, and worthy of remembering; this was the emotional challenge posed to confraternity members. While the Bible offered some detail, devotional writings, like the *Meditations on the Life of Christ,* offered elaborate detail. Works of art were inspired by the chapters of the *Meditations* and poetry too.[21] By the end of the thirteenth century there is ever more explicit emphasis on suffering, and on Jewish guilt. The *Donna de Paradiso (Lady of Paradise)*, a devotional poem composed by the Franciscan Jacopone da Todi (1230–1306), was used by many confraternities, copied into their chant books.[22] It explored Mary's pain as she witnessed the machinations of the crowd calling for Christ's death. Here are scenes never recounted in scripture, nor even offered for meditation so explicitly in the *Meditations;* here is a heightening of the temperature, a conflagration which calls for revulsion, anger and a desire for revenge. The drama is enlivened in this poem by the dramatic form in which figures speak to each other, and especially Mary and her son. Mary is told of her son's death, she is the witness to it, and hears the Jews cry.

> "Crucify him, crucify him,
> the man who pretends to be king."[23]

Mary expresses her mother's torment in alliterative mother language:

> "O son, son, son,
> son, beloved jewel!

> Son, who will console
> my anguished heart?
>
> Son, happy eyes,
> Son, why don't you answer?
>
> Son, why do you hide from
> the breast where you fed?"[24]

The book of the *laudesi* of Urbino was organized around points for contemplation. The section on Mary's pain expresses a love of the suffering body:

> To my glorious Son,
> sweeter than honey, were given
> myrrh, vinegar and bile.
> He was nailed to the cross,
> the sweet Emmanuel,
> and the cruel people
> gave him even more bitterness.[25]

Vernacular works such as this—passionate and graphic—were highly affecting. The drama was enacted between Mary and her Son, with John looking on and in the presence of the baying *popolo*—the Jews. Here is the version used by the flagellant society of Urbino, copied into its book of Marian chants:

> Cry, earth, cry sea
> cry the swimming fish;
> cry beasts in the pasture
> cry birds in their flight.
> …
> Cry the good, cry the bad
> cry people, all the same.
> The celestial God has died
> and not of a natural death.
>
> Dead is the light and its splendor
> dead the manna of great sweetness;
> of amber and muscat the odor is dead
> of roses and snow, the color is dead.[26]

In turn, Jesus himself suffers as he hears his mother's lament: "Mamma, your lament torments me like a knife." Mary speaks her sorrow to the assembled, and thus animates their devotion: "You who love the Creator, now listen to my pain."[27]

New ways of experiencing Mary and the Passion were evolving in the vernacular usages of confraternities. The men charged with writing, guiding, composing and directing the performance of compassion clearly judged the graphic telling of the Passion through Mary's eyes to be moving, effective and appealing. Texts and images put Mary center stage; they showed her suffering as only a mother can suffer over her son. They also increasingly singled out the Jews as the guilty cause for Mary's terrible pain.

The Italian confraternities probably developed the most affective techniques for imitation of the Passion, supported by a multitude of professional facilitators and expressed in image, poetic rhythm, bodily response and human voice. Such styles of collective devotion never developed in England, for example. Even a Franciscan scholar and preacher like the German Marquard of Lindau (d. 1392), wrote German sermons which treated the Passion in a much more didactic manner. His sermon on Good Friday, for example, tells the story of the Passion, but links it tightly with the promise of redemption, based on the details of the gospel story, and on authoritative homiletics, such as the writings of Bernard of Clairvaux.[28] The listener is invited to learn and appreciate the unfolding of a powerful drama of salvation, but there is far less call to join in and relive—be compassionate, feel with—the scene of the Passion. Preachers could not, of course, fully predict or control the responses to their words, but they provided cues;[29] the emotional cues of Marquard seem quite different. In our thinking about devotion and emotion, we must aim to understand the varieties of devotional styles and related emotional experiences.

* * *

I hope to have demonstrated through image and word, the creation of a world of affect, which both visualized emotion and invited response. Be it the tender embraces of mother and child or the mournful lament of a mother bereaved, the images and practices around Mary created possibilities of "emotional communities" and educated people in public participation. The symbol of nurture and symbol of loss, with her son from cradle to early grave, Mary encompassed life experiences in the language intimately used in the domestic spheres of work and education. Here was a European sentimental education which also marked indelibly those who were not formed by its rhythms and sensibilities—Mary's enemies, such as Jews and Protestants—as flawed humans without a heart.

Notes

[1] Some of Rachel Fulton's recent work on the practices and experiences of prayer are now available in "Praying by Numbers," *Studies in Medieval and Renaissance History*, third series 4(2007), pp. 195–250 and "Praying with Anselm at Admont: A Meditation on Practice," *Speculum* 81(2006), pp. 700–33.

[2] Mary Jane Morrow, "Sharing Texts: Anselmian Prayers, a Nunnery's Psalter, and the Role of Friendship," in *Voices in Dialogue. Reading Women in the Middle Ages,* ed. Linda Olson and Kathryn Kerby-Fulton, Notre Dame (IN), 2005, pp. 97–113; see figure 2, p. 100.

[3] Notre-Dame de la Belle-Verrière, first window in the aisle of the choir, south side.

[4] See Virgin and Child in the church of Estables (Lozère); Elizabeth Saxon, *The Eucharist in Romanesque France: Iconography and Theology,* Woodbridge, 2006, p. 290.

[5] Paul Binski, *Becket's Crown Art and Imagination in Gothic England 1170–1300,* London and New Haven (CN), 2004, pp. 232-5.

[6] Suzanne Lewis, *The Art of Matthew Paris in the Chronica Majora*, Cambridge, 1987, frontispiece; Paul Binski "The Faces of Christ in Matthew Paris's Chronica Majora," *Tributes in Honor of James H. Marrow: Studies in Painting and Manuscript Illumination of the late Middle Ages and Northern Renaissance*, ed. Jeffrey F. Hamburger and Anne S. Korteweg, London, 2006, pp. 85–92.

[7] We are now fortunate in the new edition, translation and performance CD of Frauenlonb's *Song of Songs* in Barbara Newman, *Frauenlob's Song of Songs,* University Park (PA), 2006, pp. 2–3:

Ei, ich sach in dem trone
ein vrouwen, die war swanger.
die trug ein wunderkrone

vor miner ougen anger.
Sie wolte wesen enbunden
sust gie die allerbeste.
zwelf steine ich zu den stunden
kos in der krone veste.

8   wie wol er mich erkande,
    der sich so vaste in mich versloz!
    wer leit mich in der liljen tal,
    da min amis curtois sich tougen in verstal?
    ich binz der sal,
    dar inne man daz gespreche man um Evan val,
    schone ich daz hal.
    secht, lieben, secht:
    min morgenröte hat erwecket
    hohen sang und richen schal,
    den niuwen tag der alten ancht,

Frauenlob's Song of Songs, pp. 22–23; lines 19–29.

[9] For some very interesting reflections see Karl F. Morrison, *The Mimetic Tradition of Reform in the West*, Princeton (NJ), 1982; for some ideas inspired by the study of Passion plays see Véronique Dominguez, *La scène et la Croix: le jeu de l'acteur dans les Passions dramatqiues françaises (XIVe-XVIe siècles)*, Texte, codex & contexte 2, Turnhout, 2007, esp. chapter 2.

[10] Just how much could go "wrong" in making the crucifix is made evident from the episode discussed in Binski, *Becket's Crown*, pp. 201-5.

[11] *Iohannis de Caulibus Meditaciones Vite Christi olim S. Bonaventuo attributae*, ed. M. Stallings-Taney, CCCM 153,

Turnhout, 1997; on Franciscan Passion poetry see F. J. E. Raby, *History of Christian-Latin Poetry from the Beginnings to the Close of the Middle Ages,* London, 1953, chapter XIII, especially pp. 429–43.

[12] "Videtur autem michi posse non incongrue dici quod non solum illa penalis et mortalis crucifixio Domini, sed ea que precesserunt eandem sunt uehementissime compassionis, amaritudinis et stuporis," *Iohannis de Caulibus Meditaciones,* c. LXXIV, pp. 252–5; at p. 253.

[13] "Non enim sibi datur uel modica requies. Sed in quali bello et conflictu, audi et uide. Alius enim apprehendit; alius ligat; alius insurgit, et alius exclamat; alius inpellit, alius blasphemat; alius expuit in eum, alius uexat; alius circumuoluit, alius interrogat; alius contra eum falsos inquirit testes, alius inquirentes associat; alius contra eum falsum testimonium dicit, alius accusat; alius deludit, alius occulos uelat; alius faciem cedit, alius colaphizat; alius eum ad columpnam ducit, alius expoliat; alius, dum ducitur, percutit, alius uociferat, alius eum insultanter ad uexandum suscipit, alius ad columpnam ligat; alius in eum impetum facit, alius flagellat; alius eum purpuram in contumeliam uestit, alius eum spinis coronat; alius arundinem in manu eius point; alius furibunde reaccipit ut spinosum capud feriat; alius nugatory genuflectit, alius sed alii plurimi intulerunt," *Ibid.*

[14] Rendered by me into modern English from *Middle English Marian Lyrics,* ed. Karen Saupe, Kalamazoo (MI), 1998, no. 36, pp. 90–91.

[15] Bram Kempers, "Icons, Altarpieces, and Civic Ritual in Siena Cathedral, 1100–1530," in *City and Spectacle in Medieval Europe,* ed. Barbara A. Hanawalt and Kathryn L. Reyerson, Minneapolis, 1994, pp. 89–136.

[16] The space has been recently excavated and the paintings revealed, and made accessible since 2004; see *Sotto il Duomo di Siena*, ed. Roberto Guerrini and Max Seidel, Milan, 2003.

[17] "Recent Acquisitions. A Selection: 2004–2005," *The Metropolitan Museum of Art Bulletin* (Fall 2005), pp. 14–15.

[18] On this image see Beth Williamson, "The Virgin *Lactans* as Second Eve: Image of the *Salvatrix*," *Studies in Iconography* 19(1998), pp. 105–38; at pp. 116–18.

[19] Hochschul- und Landesbibliothek Fulda Aa 32, fol. 71v.

[20] See for example the illumination in a mid-thirteenth-century manuscript of Welsh law, Oxford Bodleian Library, Rawlinson C821; Peter Lord, *The Visual Culture of Wales: medieval Vision,* Cardiff, 2003, figure 268, pp. 172–3.

[21] See some illuminating discussion in Anne Derbes, *Picturing the Passion in Late Medieval Italy: Narrative Painting, Franciscan Ideologies, and the Levant*, Cambridge, 1996; also Amy Neff, "The Pain of *Compassio*: Mary's Labor at the Foot of the Cross," *Art Bulletin* 80(1998), pp. 254–73.

[22] Iacopone da Todi, *Laude,* ed. Ferdinando Pappalardo, Bari, 2006, no. 70, pp. 222–7.

[23] "*Crucifige, crucifige!*
Omo che se fa rege,"
Ibid, lines 28–9, p. 223.

[24] "O figlio, figlio, figlio,
figlio, amoroso giglio!
Figlio, chi dà consiglio
al cor me' angustïato?

Figlio occhi iocundi
figlio, co' non respundi?

    Figlio, perché t'ascundi
    al petto o' si lattato?,"
Ibid, lines 40–47, p. 223.
[25] "Almio fillo beato
    Dulçe plu ke lo mele.
    Abbreuar li fo dato
    Mirra aceto effele.
    Era incroce clauato
    Lo dulçe emanuele
    Ela gente crudele
    Lidava plu amarore."
Giulio Grimaldi, "I Laudario de Disciplinati di S. Croce di Urbino," *Studj Romanzi* 12(1915), p. 9.
[26] "Planga la terra. Planga lo mare. Planga lo pesce kesa motare. Plangan le beste nel pascolare. Plangan laucelli nel lor uolare.
Planga lo bene. Planga lo male. Planga la gente. Tucta ad uguale. Morte lo rege celestiale, enno de morte sua naturale. Morte lo lume. Elo splendore. Morte lo manna delgran dulçore. Danbra emmoscato mortellodore. De neue errose morte el colore," *Ibid.*, pp. 1–96; no. 10, pp. 13–15; stanza 1, 4 and 5, pp. 13–14.
[27] "Mamma lo planto keffai
    Sinne uno coltello
    Kettucto me ua tormentando," *Ibid,* p. 21, 15/1; and "Vui kea mate lo creatore/ Ora intendate lo mio dolore," p. 15, 11/1.
[28] Rüdiger Blumrich, *Marquard von Lindau: deutsche Predigten,* Tübingen, 1994, sermon 10, pp. 87–99.
[29] On the effect of preaching performance see discussions in the forthcoming volume *Charisma and Religious Authority:*

Jewish, Christian, and Muslim Preaching 1200–1500, ed. Katherine L. Jansen and Miri Rubin, Europe Sacra 4, Turnhout, forthcoming in 2010.

Index

Abulafia, David, 38
akathistos, 21
Amiens Cathedral
    sermon for, 50–53, Figure 1
Anselm of Canterbury, 54, 83, 84
Anselm of Lucca, 83
apocrypha, 13–14

Baxendall, Michael, 8
Bartlett, Robert
    The Making of Europe, 16
Belting, Hans, 8
Bern, 27
Bernard of Clairvaux, 103
Bernardino da Siena, 13
Boynton, Susan, 21
Burkhart, Louise, 34–5

Camille, Michael, 8
Cantigas de Santa Maria, 60–63
Central European University, 20
Chartres, cathedral and school, 85
Cluny, 17–19
Confraternities
    Modena, 64–5
    Urbino *laudesi,* 101–102
Cristin, Olivier, 29
Crucifix, 64, Figure 2

Daniele da Norsa, 67–8
Davis, Natalie Zemon, 1–2, 6–7, 12, 45, 79
Devotio moderna, 26
Duccio di Buoninsegna, 96–7, Figure 8
Duffy, Eamon, 9

Elias, Norbert, 81
Eurasia, 10–11

Farmer, Sharon, 38
Fassler, Margot, 21
Foucault, Michel, 80
Francis of Assisi, 63
Franciscans, 64, 93, 103–104
    Hungarian, 66
Frauenlob (Henry of Meissen), 88–9

Gautier de Coinci
    Miracles de Nostre Dame, 5, 69
Gilbert Crispin, 54
Giotto, 64, Figure 3
Giovanni Fei, 96–7, Figure 9
Gospels, 14
Guibert of Nogent, 54
Gumppenberg, Wilhelm
    Idea Atlantis Mariani, 29–30
Gurevich, Aron, 36

Hamburger, Jeffrey, 9
Hildegard of Bingen, 22–23

Huizinga, Johann, 25
Hungary, 17–19
hymns, 24–5

identity, chapter 2, esp. 45–8
Isis, 15

Jacopone da Todi
    Donna de paradiso, 100–101
Jean Gerson, 13
Jews, 13, 38, 48–9, 53–61, 66–9, 100–103, 104
Johannes Gobi
    Scala Coeli, 35

Klaniczay, Gábor, 17
Koerner, Joseph, 9

Lanyer, Amelia
    'Salutation and Sorrow of the Virgine Mary', 28–9
Luther, Martin, 23–5

MacCormack, Sabina, 38
Magnificat, 21, 23–5
Mantegna, Andrea
    Madonna of Victory, 67
Marquard of Lindau, 103–104
Mary, *passim*
    images: mother and child, Figures 6, 7 and 8
    lactans, 96–7, Figure 8
    sedes sapientiae, 85, Figure 5

theotokos 85
Matthew Paris
    Chronica majora, 87
Meditations on the Life of Christ, 91–3, 99–100
miracle tales, Marian, 34–5, 56–63, 68–9
monasteries and monastic culture, 17–18, 22–3, 55–6, 84–7
Moore, R. I.
    The Formation of a Persecuting Society, 49
Mosquera, Daniel, 36
Muslims, 62–3

Nahuatl religion lore, 34–6
New Spain, 31–4, 37
    Franciscans in, 32–3
Newman, Barbara, 23
Nussbaum, Martha, 80

Odo of Tournai
    On Original Sin, 54–5

Page, Christopher, 22
Passion, representation of, 87, 89–104, Figures 2, 10 and 11
periodization, 25–7
Pietà, 80
Protestants, 23–5, 104
Purgatory, 82–3

Regensburg, 68, Figure 4
Reuter, Timothy, 11–12
Robertson, Anne Walters, 21

Salve regina, 21
Savonarola, Girolamo, 13
Shaftesbury, nunnery, 84
shrines
    Chartres, 16
    Copanahuastla (diocese of Chiapas), 37
    Loreto, 16
    Oberbüren, 27
    Rocamadour, 16
Siena, art, 95–7
Soergel, Philip, 29

Theotokos, 85
Throne of Wisdom (*sedes sapientiae*), 85, Figure 5
Toledo cathedral, 85

Vincent Ferrer, 13

Wallace, David, 39
Wright, Craig, 21

Pictures

1. Amiens Cathedral, West façade, 1260s
2. Cimabue: Crucifix
   Florence, Museo dell'Opera di Santa Croce
3. Giotto: Lamentation of Christ, 1305–06
   Scrovegni Chapel, Padova
4. Regensburg, Schöne Maria
   Coburg, Kunstsammlung der Veste
5. Seat of Wisdom Mother of God, of Ger, Wooden statue
   Barcelona, Museu Nacional d'Art de Catalunya, second half of 12th century
6. Enthroned Virgin and Child, c. 1260–1280
   French, made in Paris, elephant ivory with traces of paint and gilding New York, Metropolitan Museum of Art, The Cloisters Collection
7. Maestro di Tressa: Madonna degli occhi grossi, early 13th century
   Siena, Opera della Metropolitana, aut no. 1341/08
8. Duccio di Buoninsegna: Madonna and Child
   New York, Metropolitan Museum of Art
9. Paolo di Giovanni Fei: Madonna del latte
   Siena, Opera della Metropolitana aut. no. 1019, III, 6. Foto LENSINI Siena.
10. Venetian Artist, Diptych, mid-14th century
    Tempera and gold on wood, right panel: 35.5x24.2 cm; left panel: 35.5x24 cm
    Esztergom, Christian Museum
11. Thomas of Coloswar (active in the 1420, probably in Buda), Crucifixion altarpiece, 1427
    Tempera and gold on wood central field: 242 x 177 cm
    Esztergom, Christian Museum

1.

2.

3.

4.

5.

6.

7.

8.

9.

10.

11.

Milton Keynes UK
Ingram Content Group UK Ltd.
UKHW031322030924
447832UK00019B/240

9 789639 776364